SILVERTOWN

AND NEIGHBOURHOOD

(INCLUDING EAST AND WEST HAM)

A RETROSPECT

BY

ARCHER PHILIP CROUCH

AUTHOR OF "SEÑORITA MONTENAR," "FOR THE REBEL CAUSE," ETC.

LONDON

THOMAS BURLEIGH

1900

PREFACE.

IT would be impossible for the author, within the brief
limits of a preface, to make an acknowledgment of all the
persons and books he has consulted in the course of writing
the present small volume.   The names of both will be
found, as the references occur, in the body of the book,
but amongst them should be mentioned here those of
Mr. Thomas Mathews, formerly of East Ham, who gave
the author much information concerning the neighbourhood; Dr. G. Pagenstecher, who wrote the "Story of West
Ham Park," and compiled Miss Fry's "History of East
and West Ham"; and Mr. J. S. Curwen, author of "Old
Plaistow."   Special acknowledgment is due to Mr.
C. R. Wylie, who kindly supplied the greater number
of the photographs.

LIST OF ILLUSTRATIONS.

CONTENTS.

❁

CHAPTER I.

CHAPTER II.

CHAPTER III.

CHAPTER IV.

CHAPTER V.

CHAPTER VI.

CHAPTER VII.

CHAPTER VIII.

CHAPTER IX.

CHAPTER X.

Silvertown and Neighbourhood.

CHAPTER I.

The Half-Hundred of Becontree—Barking Abbey—Bow Bridge—
Stratford Langthorne Abbey—Stratford.

SILVERTOWN, so called from Mr. Silver's factory, now the
property of the India-rubber, Gutta-percha, and Telegraph Works Company, Limited, is an outlying district
of the Borough of West Ham, forming part of an island cut
off by the Victoria and Albert Docks on the west, north, and
east, and by the River Thames on the south. In the year
1850 Silvertown did not exist, and West Ham was a small
and practically unknown suburban district in the east of
London, with barely 18,000 inhabitants. In 1900 Silvertown has the population of a fairly large country town, and
West Ham, created a borough within the last few years,
boasts of some 300,000 inhabitants, being the eighth largest
town in England, and exceeding the population of several
European capitals. The record of such a marvellous growth
may not be devoid of interest.

The borough of West Ham, and the urban district of
East Ham—a modern village of nearly 90,000 inhabitants—
occupy, with the exception of two small portions in the
south-east corner belonging respectively to Kent and
Barking, the whole of the space between the River Lea
and the River Roding. On the north they are bounded by
Leyton and Wanstead ; on the south by the River Thames.

East and West Ham derive their name from an old village
called "Hamme," which was included in the East Anglia
which King Alfred ceded in 878 to Guthrum the Dane.
The village also appears in Doomsday Book in reference to

a gift by Edward the Confessor of "two Hides in Hamme " (a hide equals a hundred acres) to the Abbot of West-minster. These two hides included the land on which the North Woolwich Gardens now stand.

The two Hams lie in the Half-hundred of Becontree, to which also belong Barking, Dagenham, Great and Little Ilford, Leyton, Wanstead, Woodford and Walthamstow. The name of Becontree, according to Philip Morant, M.A., Rector of St. Mary's, Colchester, who published a history of Essex in 1768, owes its origin to a beacon which used to stand on Windmill Hill at Woodford. "Such beacons," the historian observes, "were a precaution necessary before the increase of our naval strength made us masters of the sea." This remark struck two succeeding historians of Essex, Peter Muilman and Sir H. B. Dudley, as being so apt, that hey both quoted it, neglecting, however, to mention the source from which they had derived it.

There seems to have been an epidemic of Essex historians towards the end of the eighteenth century. Salmon, who brought out his history in 1760, incited no less than three men to attempt to outvie his performance. Morant's history appeared in 1768, Muilman's in 1770, and Sir H. B. Dudley's in 1772. Forty years had elapsed from Cox's history in 1720 to Salmon's history in 1760, and another forty years passed from Dudley's history in 1772 to Elizabeth Ogborne's in 1812. A curious fact is that Sir H. B. Dudley dedicated his work to Peter Muilman without knowing that he was a rival in the same field, for Muilman's history was published at first under the *nom de guerre* of a "gentleman."

At one time the whole Half-hundred of Becontree, some thirty miles in circumference, belonged to Barking Abbey, which was the oldest and richest nunnery in England Indeed, the early history of Barking, which is only three miles from Silvertown, is the history of this nunnery, and the town rose to importance and declined with the rise and fall of its Abbey. Founded in 670, Ethelburgh, sister of the Bishop of London, became the first abbess of the convent. In 870 the Abbey was burnt to the ground by the Danes. Situated on the banks of the Roding, it lay at the mercy of these marauders, and for a period of one hundred years no attempt was made to rebuild it. At length King Edgar, moved to remorse by having violated the beautiful nun Wulfhilda of Wilton, tried to make atonement by restoring the Abbey and placing her at the head of it. When he died, his widow Elfrida, actuated no doubt by jealousy, turned her out of the Abbey and took possession of her post.

Barking next appears in history as the town to which William the Conqueror withdrew after the battle of Hastings, waiting there while the Tower of London was being built for his occupation. The name of Barking has been derived by some from *Beorce*, a birch, and *ing*, a meadow; by others, from *Burgh*, a fortification, and *ing*, a meadow. The fact that it had to be protected against the attacks of the Danes makes the latter derivation the most probable, as well as its selection by William the Conqueror for his military base. Here he received the submission of Edgar Atheling, the Saxon heir to the throne, and accepted homage from Edwin, Earl of Mercia, and Morcar, Earl of Northumberland. Some meadows in East Ham, on the right bank of the river Roding, where he is said to have met a deputation from London, are called to this day " Parly Marshes."

Barking Abbey was dedicated to the Virgin Mary, and the nuns belonged to the Benedictine order. The Abbess was one of four abbesses who were baronesses by virtue of the posts they held, though, of course, their sex prevented them taking a seat in the House of Lords. The other three Abbeys were Wilton, Shaftesbury, and St. Mary's, Winchester, Barking taking precedence over all of them. The Abbess lived in great state, her household consisting of several chaplains, an esquire, gentlemen-in-waiting, yeomen, grooms, and numerous male attendants. The distinction of the position may be gathered from the fact that three Queens of England—Elfrida, widow of Edgar, Maud, Queen of Henry I., and Matilda, Queen of Stephen—were proud to hold it.

Amongst the privileges of the Abbess of Barking was permission to keep dogs for hunting hares and foxes in Essex. In those early days, ladies who took the veil, instead of immuring themselves in the cloister, often led a jolly, open-air existence, many of them becoming ardent sportswomen. One of the first treatises on hunting, hawking and fishing was written by Julia de Berners, Prioress of

Sopewell, near St. Albans, "a gentlewoman endowed with great gifts of body and mind." This Julia de Berners may frequently have been asked over to Barking by the Abbess for a "run with the Abbey hounds." On occasions, when the fox took a southerly course, they would cross the "two hides" belonging to the Abbot of Westminster. The Abbot might, at the time, have been engaged in the pastime of hawking amidst the wild fowl which haunted the river marshes. Apologies would be made to him, a few compliments would doubtless pass, and then, after exchanging notes with regard to the day's sport, the ladies would ride on.

The later history of Barking Abbey is somewhat uneventful. In 1376, owing to a breach in the river wall on the left bank of the Thames at Dagenham, a short distance east of Barking Creek, the Abbey was flooded. The inundations recurred in 1380 and 1382, but, at considerable expense to the Convent, works were at length undertaken which removed any further fear of trouble from this cause. At the dissolution of Monasteries in 1539 the Abbey surrendered to the Crown, and the demesne lands were leased by Henry VIII. to Sir Thomas Dennye. On the list of abbesses is to be found the name of Mary à Beckett, sister of the Archbishop of Canterbury, and among illustrious personages who have resided there may be mentioned Eleanor, widow of the murdered Duke of Gloucester. When Catherine de la Pole, daughter of the Earl of Suffolk, was abbess, Edmund, Earl of Richmond (father of Henry VII.), and Jasper, Earl of Pembroke, sons of Owen Tudor by Catherine, the Queen-Dowager, were educated in the abbey.

The site of Barking Abbey is close to the parish church, and the Abbey Church, the foundations of which were traced by Smart Lethieullier, the antiquarian, ran parallel to it. Access is gained to the present church under the arch of a tower which is generally known as " Fire Bell Gate." It is plain from records that this tower was a portion of the Abbey, though some antiquarians continue to deny it. It is the only portion of the Abbey which still stands. The gateway possesses a single room, which is called " The Chapel of the Holy Rood Loft at the Gate."

Photo by Alfred Scott.

West Ham Park.

[Stratford.

[To face p. 10.

In one corner of the room, on the side which faces east, is a representation in stone of the "holy rood" or crucifixion. In the upper story a bell used to hang, which was in all probability the curfew of the Conqueror's time. It has long since been removed, from fear, no doubt, of endangering the tower.

Mention has already been made of the connection of King Henry the First's consort with Barking Abbey. Queen Maud, or Matilda, as she seems to have been indifferently called, had taken the veil as a young girl, and according to some historians was so devoted to conventual life that she did not wish to leave it, even to be Queen of England. Others give a different account of her, and Sharon Turner, in his English History, relates that when Anselm, Archbishop of Canterbury, declared she could not marry the King on account of the vows she had taken, her answer was both vigorous and convincing. "I do not deny," she said, "that I have worn the veil, for when I was a child my friend Christiana "—this was her aunt, the Abbess of Wilton—" put a black cloth on my head to preserve me from outrage. When I used to throw it off, she would torment me with harsh blows and indecent reproaches. Sighing and trembling I have worn it in her presence, but as soon as I could withdraw from her sight I always threw it on the ground and trampled it under foot. When my father saw me once in it he tore it from me in a great rage, and execrated the person who had first put it on." The young girl's tastes evidently lay with the glitter of the Court, in preference to the gloom of the convent.

Although Matilda did not care to be an inmate of a nunnery she had no objection to ruling one, and as abbess or directress of Barking Abbey made frequent visits to the convent. Her route lay along the old Roman road, commencing with Old Street and passing through Bethnal Green over the river Lea at the Old Ford. This ford was crossed by a ferry, which in times of flood became very difficult to manage. An accident which happened to the Queen herself at this spot led to the building of Bow Bridge, and, incidentally, to the birth of Stratford itself. This is what John Stow says of the matter in his "Survey of London," published in 1598. "Matilda, when she saw the way to bee dangerous to them yt travailed by the old foord over the river of Lue (for she herselfe had beene well washed* in the water), caused two stone bridges to be builded in a place one mile distant from the old foord, of the which, one was situated over Lue at the head of the towne of Stratford now called Bow, a rare piece of worke, for before that time the like had never beene seen in England; the other over the little brooke comonly called Chanelsebridge."

This bridge spanned the Channelsea, which is a branch of the Lea, separating from it in the Hackney Marshes, and joining it again below Stratford. The Channelsea is said to be an artificial canal, which Alfred the Great cut on a certain occasion when the Danes had anchored in the Lea. The water was diverted by this channel, and the ships, left high and dry, were attacked and utterly destroyed. The site of the Channelsea Bridge is close to the present Stratford Market Station, which used to be called Stratford Bridge.

Queen Matilda's enterprise not only afforded the best route from London to the Eastern counties, but also caused two new places to spring into existence—Stratford-atte-Bowe, now Bow, on the right bank of the Lea, and Stratford Langthorne, now Stratford, on the left bank of the Lea. The first name in both cases was due of course to the fact that they were built on or near to "the Street of the Ford" (Stratford). Ships from the Continent used to sail up the Lea and discharge their passengers at the new bridge. Chaucer's mention of " Frenche after the scole of Stratford-atte-Bowe " is usually supposed to be a mocking reference to the attempts of the good people of the neighbourhood to converse with their foreign visitors. Other commentators think that the poet had in his mind a well-known ladies' seminary in the district, which, owing to its advantageous location, claimed to teach its pupils the best Parisian accent. Bow Bridge was so called from the fact of its being the first arched bridge in England. For deriving the name from the French word *beau*, as some historians do, there is no

---

* The reader must not carry away the impression, from the wording of this passage, that Queen Matilda believed, in common with certain nations of the present day, that it is dangerous to the health to be " well washed " in water.

reason except the poor one that Frenchmen used to land at the bridge, and may have applied that epithet to it.

Before the building of Bow Bridge, West Ham was a small village remote from the public highways, but the new road through the northern portion of the parish made it more accessible. It was probably this new road which led William de Montfichet to select West Ham as the locality for the Abbey which he founded in 1135, and which came to be called the Abbey of Stratford Langthorne. The monks of the abbey, like all Cistercians, were fond of horticulture, and the name Langthorne is said to be derived from the hedges of "long thorns" with which they surrounded their plots of ground. The Cistercians are so called from Citeaux, a place near Dijon, from which the monks of La Trappe originally came.

The Abbey of Stratford Langthorne, with grounds covering some sixteen acres, was the earliest, wealthiest and most pleasantly situated Cistercian house in the country. That its surroundings were ever picturesque it seems impossible to believe when one gazes to-day at the old "Adam and Eve" public house, the Abbey Mills, and the North Woolwich Railway, which now cover its site. Yet Camden in 1586 describes the Lea at Stratford as "washing the green meadows and making them look very charming," while Weaver in 1631 saw here "the remains of a Monastery pleasantly watered about with several streams, and the meadows near the mills planted round with willows." The Abbey itself was on the Channelsea, but the Lea is only half a mile distant from its site, and the scenery described by Camden must have been within easy view of the Abbey grounds.

Although Stratford Langthorne Abbey was too recent a structure to have been exposed to attacks from the Danes, it suffered considerably from a natural enemy, being flooded so frequently that the monks for a time deserted it, retiring to Burgestede (Burstead) near Billericay. During this interval, it is to be presumed, the banks of the Lea and Channelsea were strengthened, so that the monks could return to Stratford without fear of further molestation. Several kings of England are mentioned in connection with the abbey. Richard I., who is said to have repaired the buildings after the floods, granted it a charter in 1193.

Henry III. in 1267 received the Pope's legate within its walls, and in 1467 the Abbot sumptuously entertained Edward IV., who, in return for the good dinner, gave his host a grant of two casks of wine per annum. It was from this Abbey that Margaret, the aged Countess of Salisbury, in the reign of Henry VIII., was dragged to the Tower to be beheaded on a charge of treason. How she came to be living in a monastery and not a nunnery history does not explain.

At the beginning of the nineteenth century an ornamental arch of the chapel and a brick gateway giving entrance to the precincts of the Abbey were still standing. These have long since disappeared, and the only relic now lies in the Church of St. John the Evangelist at Stratford. It consists of a stone carving unearthed during the making of the North Woolwich Railway in 1845. Archdeacon Stephens, to whom the writer is indebted for these particulars, purchased it from the landlord of the "Adam and Eve" public house, in whose yard it had lain exposed to the weather for many years. The design is a number of human skulls set in separate niches, and may have been built into the wall, or stood over the door of the mortuary chapel.

During the construction of this railway an old bath, 12 ft. long by 8 ft. wide and 5 ft. deep, was also found. It consisted of an outer stone wall 6 ins. thick lined with red tiles, which again were covered with finely glazed Dutch tiles. At the same time were discovered an aqueduct leading to the river, a rough stone coffin, and an onyx seal set in silver with the words *Nuncio vobis gaudium et salutem* engraven on it. This was probably the Abbey seal.

The prosperity of Stratford was increased in 1357 by an Act of Edward the Third, ordering that cattle should not be allowed to approach nearer to London than that village. The object of the Act was to prevent disease being spread in the city by the accumulation of putrefying offal. Stratford now became the slaughter-house of the metropolis, supplying Butchers' Row with meat. Bread was also made there on a very large scale, the Abbey Mills furnishing the flour, and Epping Forest the faggots for the ovens. Stratford bakers are mentioned by Holinshed in the year 1414. In 1553 Queen Mary passed through Stratford on her way

to coronation.   Stratford has reason to remember "Bloody"
Mary, for three years later eleven men and two women were
burnt alive by her upon the village green.   The church of
St. John the Evangelist was built on this green in 1835, and
on the spot where Mary's victims suffered martyrdom a stone
memorial now stands.

CHAPTER II.

Roman Reclamation of the Marshes—East Ham Church—Greenstreet House—Queen Anne Boleyn's Tower—St. Nicolas' Industrial Schools —Ancient Penalty imposed on Tenants of East Ham.

THE marshes of East and West Ham show traces of Roman reclamation work in the counter-walls or embankments which they raised against the Thames. At Uphall, between Barking and Ilford, are to be seen the remains of a Roman encampment of such dimensions that Smart Lethieullier, the antiquarian, thought it must have been a town. He accounted for the absence of any ruins by the surmise that the building materials had all been carried away for the construction of Barking Abbey, in the foundations of which he found some Roman stones.

It is more probable, however, that Uphall was an encampment formed to hold a large body of conquered Britons, who, under the superintendence of a Roman cohort, were forced to build counter-walls for the reclamation of Plaistow and East Ham levels. They did their work well, winning the land piece by piece from the river. Mr. Thomas Mathews, once a farmer in East Ham, and still owning a good deal of property there, informed the writer that in one portion of his estate the remains of five embankments are to be found, raised one after the other against the river. To the energy of the Romans East and West Ham owe more than half their land, most of the present river-wall being of Roman origin.

Manor Way, which runs from East Ham to the river, was in all probability a Roman road, built to facilitate the reclamation of the marshes. During the construction of the Northern Outfall Sewer in 1863 some Roman coffins were found close to Manor Way. They were taken to the parish church, which stands near the spot, and were subsequently removed to the British Museum. Here they

Photo by]

[C. R. Wylie, Esq.

Old Parish Church, East Ham.

[To face p. 16.

enjoyed the distinction of being viewed amongst other Roman antiquities, till 1899, when they were consigned to the cellars, the room in which they were exhibited being required for Baron Rothschild's Waddesdon bequest of jewels and plate. It is to be feared that they will not see the light of day again.

There is reason to believe that the marshes in this district were once forest land. During the excavations for the Victoria Docks, hazel, oak, and yew-trees were found in a stratum of peat bog. The explanation that these trees were brought down the river in flood time is confuted by the fact that the greater number of them were, when unearthed, standing upright just as they had grown. Even those which lay horizontally did not support the theory. Mr. Mathews, while digging a dyke near Wall End, came upon several trees which, though horizontal, were all lying in the same direction, as though they had been swept down where they stood by an overwhelming weight of water. Amongst them were hazel trees with nuts as big as walnuts. The marshes appear to have been formed in historic times, for in the peat stratum of the Victoria Docks were found a millstone and a brass dish, while a canoe 27 feet long was dug out during the excavations for the Albert Docks.

The oldest building in East Ham is the Parish Church, which lies about two miles from Silvertown and less than a mile from the eastern end of the Albert Docks. It stands on the very edge of the marsh, and is still surrounded on three sides by fields, modern East Ham having sprung up on the firm land to the north of the Barking Road. A Saxon church probably stood on the site of the present one, which was built about the middle of the twelfth century at the expense, it is said, of two sisters, in memory of a brother who fell in the Crusades. Mr. J. T. Micklethwaite, the present surveyor of Westminster Abbey, inspected the church in 1891, and refers to it in his report as a building of unusual interest. "The churches near London," he writes, "have generally been so much altered and enlarged and rebuilt, sometimes even more than once, to meet the requirements of an always growing population, that it was a surprise to find one of them substantially in the form in

c

which it was built over seven centuries ago. Few, even amongst remote village churches, have been so little altered in their fabric as this has." Stronger testimony to the isolation of East Ham up to the beginning of the nineteenth century could not be adduced.

The walls of the church, three feet in thickness, are made of stone and flint, and the building is so small that, even with modern seats, it can only accommodate 150 people. The old pews, which have only been removed within the last few years, were spacious and lofty, many of them being provided with fireplaces, for the flues of which holes were cut in the walls. A tower stands at the western end. Mr. Mathews, who was churchwarden from 1843 to 1858, says that a peal of seven bells used to hang in this tower, but that in 1770 five of them were sold, as their ringing was thought to endanger the structure. One of the two remaining bells bears the inscription in Saxon letters, *Dulcis sisto melis, vocor campano Gabrielis.* This is supposed to state that the bell was named after the sweet-voiced Gabriel, but as the words are bastard Latin it is impossible to discover the exact meaning they were intended to convey.

A fine monument stands in the chancel to Edmund Nevill, Earl of Westmoreland. The identity of this Edmund Nevill is not easy to establish. Some consider him to be the same earl who was attainted for complicity in the rising of the north in 1570 in favour of Mary Queen of Scots, and who obtained a general pardon from Queen Elizabeth in 1585. This, however, was the 6th Earl, who died in exile and left no issue. The Edmund Nevill of East Ham was probably the grandson of the 5th Earl, through whom he claimed the estates. His application was addressed to James I. in 1605, but as he could not produce the sum which that monarch demanded in return for royal recognition he never obtained the title or the property. His monument bears the following inscription :—"To the memory of the Rt. Hon. Edmund Nevill, Lord Latimer, Earl of Westmoreland, and Dame Jane his wife, with the memorials of their seven children; which Edmund was lineally descended from the honourable blood of kings and princes, and the 7th Earl of Westmoreland of the name of Nevill." The writer of the epitaph then breaks into verse as follows :—

"From princely and from honorable blood, by true succession was my high descent.
Malignant crosses oft opposed my good, and adverse chance my state did circumvent."

Curiously enough, neither place nor date is given for his decease, though the inscription states that his wife died at Mile End in 1641. The monument represents himself and his spouse, life size, in a kneeling posture. The seven children, on a considerably smaller scale, are placed at the base of the tomb. Why this unfortunate, uncoroneted earl resided in such an out-of-the-way place as East Ham it is difficult to understand, unless he inherited property in the neighbour-hood, or was compelled to practise the most rigid economies. It is generally supposed that he lived in Greenstreet House, East Ham, a residence said to belong to the Latimers.

His widow, Dame Jane, left a yearly income of £3 to the church, to be divided into three parts : 1st, for the repair of the tomb ; 2nd, for bread and coal for the poor ; 3rd, for a sermon on John the Baptist day. The money for these benefactions was due from some property called Ox Lees, in West Ham, and was paid by its various owners till 1828. Then the executors of a late holder disputed the claim, and as there was no fund to meet the expenditure of £60 or £70 required to substantiate it, the matter was allowed to drop.

East Ham churchyard is the resting-place of the famous English antiquary, Dr. William Stukeley, who was born at Holbeach, Lincolnshire, in 1687. His early memoirs read like the "Bad Boy's Diary." At home for the holidays on one occasion he relates how he made "a handsome sceleton of an aged cat." As an undergraduate at Cambridge he "went frequently a-simpling" (collecting plants or "simples"), and ingenuously confesses having begun "to steal dogs and dissect them." In 1719 he took the medical diploma of M.D., and practised at Boston and Grantham, from which latter place he removed to London, becoming a Fellow of the Royal College of Physicians in 1720. Nine years later the doctor entered Holy Orders, abandoning, it is to be hoped, the practice of "stealing dogs" for his dissecting table. After being vicar of All Saints, Stamford, he was presented in 1747 with the living of St. George the Martyr, Queen Square, London. As a clergyman, Dr. Stukeley could not be called conventional. Preaching in spectacles for the first time at the age of seventy-six, he gave as his text, "Now we see through a glass darkly."

Dr. Stukeley's best known works are "An Account of Stonehenge and Abury" and "An Account of the Antiquities and Curiosities of Great Britain." Sir Isaac Newton was one of his most intimate friends, amongst whom could also be reckoned a clergyman not so well known to posterity, the Rev. Joseph Sims, at that time vicar of East Ham. The doctor is said to have expressed a wish to be buried near his "dear friend Sims." It was natural enough that the learned antiquarian should desire to lie within the precincts of such a venerable structure, but that he should refuse to allow a tombstone or even a mound of earth to notify his grave is more remarkable. A lifetime devoted to the study of monuments had, perhaps, convinced him of the futility of attempting to perpetuate his memory by such ineffectual means.

The doctor's instructions were carried out, and the only evidence of his having been buried in the churchyard was an entry in the register in the handwriting of Mr. Sims under the year 1765. It runs: "Rev. Dr. Stukeley, late rector of St. George's, Queen Square, March 9." The Penny Encyclopædia of 1842 says: "No antiquarian ever had so lively, not to say licentious, a fancy as Stukeley. The idea of the obscure, remote past inflamed him like a passion; most even of his descriptions are rather visions than sober relations of what would be perceived by an ordinary eye; and never before or since were such broad continuous webs of speculation woven out of little more than moonshine." The latest edition of the "Dictionary of National Biography" states that Gibbon the historian acknowledged having used Dr. Stukeley's materials, though he rejected his fanciful conjectures. Bishop Warburton described the doctor as "a strange compound of simplicity, drollery, absurdity, ingenuity, superstition, and antiquarianism." Thomas Hearne, whoever he may be, calls him "a mighty conceited man." Whether this epithet is to be taken in its modern uncomplimentary sense, or merely means that he was a man of much imagination, the writer of the biographical article leaves his readers to determine for themselves.

The sequel to the story of Dr. Stukeley's unostentatious burial is somewhat interesting. In March, 1886, according to the "East Ham Almanack," the sexton's son was digging a grave in what he thought to be a vacant space, when he discovered a coffin about 6 ft. below the surface. The coffin was in good preservation, with an embossed plate of brass beautifully ornamented with scroll work, surmounted by a goat's head, and bearing the following inscription :—

. . . . Diis
Rev. Gulielmus Stukeley, M.D.
Obiit Tertes Die Martii
1765.
Ætatis suæ 77 ans.*

The coffin lay side by side with another one, which was discovered to be, not that of his "dear friend" Sims, next to whom he wished to be buried, but that of his "dear friend's" wife, who died Sept. 17th, 1768. The grave of the husband, who was buried eight years later, lies some yards away to the westward of the couple.

The oldest house in East Ham is probably Greenstreet House, in Green Street, the supposed residence of Edmund Nevill, and now portion of a Roman Catholic Reformatory for boys. This house is said to have originally belonged to the Boleyns, who had estates in Essex. The tower which stands in the grounds is still called "Queen Anne Boleyn's Tower." The story is that when King Henry VIII. first thought of making her his queen, she had just lost a young nobleman to whom she was betrothed. In such cases it was the custom for a girl to remain in mourning for twelve months, and the king, for her entertainment during this period of seclusion, built the tower, from which she could see the shipping on the "Thames" and the distant hills of Kent.

---

* The spelling is obviously incorrect, but might pass when allowance is made for the difficulty of deciphering a plate which has been underground for more than a hundred years.

That the tower had once belonged to someone in a
position to indulge extravagant tastes is plain, from the fact
that the room in the third storey was originally lined with
leather inlaid with gold.　So costly a covering accords well
with the popular conception of the hero of the Field of the
Cloth of Gold.　A Mr. Morley, who lived in the house at the
beginning of the nineteenth century, says that, according to
a history of England which he had read, Henry VIII., on
his suspicions being aroused with regard to her, had Queen
Anne confined in the same tower in which five years previously he had courted her.　From here she was taken by
water, down Ham Creek—which ran almost up to the house
—to Greenwich, and thence to the Tower of London.

In his "Environs of London," published in 1796, Lysons,
usually a reliable authority, disposes of the story with the
remark that "the tower is evidently of more recent date."
But this judgment was delivered after only a hurried inspection of the building, the modern appearance of which
Mr. Morley explained to two antiquarians who visited it in
1824.　An account of this visit by one of them is to be
found in the *Gentleman's Magazine* for March in that year.
Mr. Morley told them that his predecessor had not only cut
up the leather wall-covering for the sake of the gold, which
realised £30, but that he had also sold the lead from the
roof, so that the two upper stories of the tower had fallen
into decay.　Mr. Morley had them pulled down, and protected the other three with a new copper roof.　This had
given Lysons the idea that the structure was a modern one.
In further support of the local tradition, Mr. Morley assured
the writer of the article in the *Gentleman's Magazine* that he
had himself seen a letter in the handwriting of King
Henry VIII. dated from Greenstreet.

Greenstreet House remained in Mr. Morley's family till
1869, when it was bought by Cardinal Manning and devoted
to its present purpose.　The old house and tower remain
unaltered, but large additions have been made at the rear of
the former.　The old-world garden, surrounded by lofty
red-brick walls, is gradually losing the magnificent cedars
which used to adorn it.　The drainage of the new streets
which have sprung up around it has drawn off the water
necessary for their sustenance.　Even the large fish-pond

Queen Anne Boleyn's Tower, Greenstreet House,
East Ham.

[To face p. 22

at the end of the garden, where the present rector of the
Reformatory remembers catching, some thirty years ago, as
many as eighty fish in one afternoon, has nearly run dry.
It is possible that the heavy rates levied on the property
will prevent its present owners from remaining in possession
of it. If so, the fine old red-brick mansion with its historic
memories will be pulled down, and on its site new streets
will rise in dull uniformity with those of the surrounding
district.

Another old East Ham Manor House is also held by
Roman Catholics. This is the Manor of East Ham Burnels,
which lies to the north of the Romford Road, and from which
the district of Manor Park derives its name. It now forms
a portion of the St. Nicolas Industrial Schools. The original
Manor House of East Ham was the old East Ham Hall,
which stood near the church and was only pulled down in
December 1899. The demesne lands of this manor were
considerable, and an old boundary stone still stands at the
side of the Barking Road almost as far as the "Duke's
Head" at Wall End, on which is inscribed "Manor of East
Ham Hall." In 1286 Bishop Burnel of Bath and Wells
bought land in East and West Ham, which came to be
called the Manor of Burnels. This manor was afterwards
divided into East Ham Burnels and West Ham Burnels,
the former being the St. Nicolas Industrial Schools and the
latter the manor house, which Sir Henry Pelly occupied, just
opposite the south-east corner of West Ham Park.

The Manor House, which is now included in the
St. Nicolas Industrial Schools, was bought by Cardinal
Manning in 1868. The estate had been a large one, the
carriage drive running down through an avenue of trees to
a lodge on the Romford Road. The Cardinal had been in
treaty for its purchase some years previously but had
thought the price too high, and a land company bought it
The rapid appreciation of property in this district may be
gathered from the fact that he subsequently paid for the
house alone the same sum for which the whole estate had
previously been offered to him. The house, a fine old
country mansion, was once the residence of Mr. Fry, the
husband of Elizabeth Fry, the celebrated prison reformer.
They belonged to the Society of Friends as they call

themselves, or Quakers as others call them. It may not be generally known that the latter name is derived from the fact that George Fox, the founder of the sect, when brought before the magistrate replied to his strictures by bidding him "tremble and quake at the name of the Lord."

Almost every history of Essex states that the tenants of the Manor of East Ham were obliged to "treat and entertain" the tenants of the Manors of West Ham, West Ham Burnels, and Plaiz (Plaistow), according to injunctions laid upon them by a former lord of the manor. They had refused to pay his ransom when made a prisoner of war, and having presumably raised the money elsewhere he returned and took this means of having his revenge upon them. No information is given in the earlier histories as to the manner in which the custom was observed, and the reader was left to suppose that whenever a tenant of West Ham, West Ham Burnels, and Plaiz felt inclined for a good meal, he had only to walk to East Ham to get it. A later chronicler, however, states that the "treating could only be demanded on days when the manorial court sat at East Ham"—once, perhaps, in every three weeks—so that the advantages to be derived by the tenants of the other manors were not so great as they first appeared. The custom survived till the middle of the eighteenth century.

CHAPTER III.

Little Ilford—History of Wanstead House.

LITTLE ILFORD, now included in the Urban District of East Ham, and lying on the right bank of the River Roding, possesses an interesting little church, parts of which are 900 years old. The building holds some 130 persons, and for eight centuries—down to the beginning of Queen Victoria's reign—the accommodation was ample for its parishioners, who in that time never exceeded 160 souls. They are now increased a hundred fold, the present population being 16,000. A monument to William, Earl Waldegrave, who died in 1610, stands in the chancel, and the vestry, which is the oldest part of the church, contains the memorials of the Lethieullier family, including Smart Lethieullier, the antiquarian, who died in 1760.

The family residence of the Lethieulliers was Aldersbrook Manor, on the site of which, to the west of Wanstead Flats, the City of London Cemetery now stands. The beauty of the cemetery is due to the care with which the Manor grounds were laid out and tended. In 1754 Smart Lethieullier bought the Manor of Barking from the Fanshawes for £60,000. If the manor included no more land than when Thomas Fanshawe paid King Charles I. £2,000 for it in 1628, the appreciation of the property must have been great indeed. Peter Muilman, the Essex historian already mentioned, says that in 1770 Little Ilford consisted of one street, "where citizens go on a Sunday for an airing." If they had gone for beautiful scenery, they would have met with disappointment, for the country is perfectly flat for miles.

Wanstead Flats cannot be mentioned without recalling Wanstead House, the pride of Essex a hundred years ago. Wanstead lies just outside the northern boundary of West

Ham, and about four miles from Silvertown. Many illustrious persons lived in the house preceding the magnificent
structure which adorned the site at the beginning of the
nineteenth century. In Henry VIII.'s reign, Sir Giles
Heron, who married Cecilia, daughter of Sir Thomas More,
owned the property. On the execution of Sir Thomas the
estate was confiscated, and in the following reign in 1549
given to Richard Rich, the solicitor-general, who, in spite of
having been a school friend of the Chancellor's, conducted
the prosecution and secured his condemnation. Rich
afterwards succeeded to his victim's office, as well as his
estate, and Campbell, in his "Lives of the Chancellors,"
justly describes him as "one of the most sordid, as well as
the most unprincipled, men who ever held the office."

At Wanstead, in August, 1553, Richard Rich entertained
Queen Mary on her way to London for her coronation.
Here, too, came Elizabeth, to pay respects to her sister.
The Chancellor, who had persecuted Roman Catholics and
extreme Protestants with great impartiality, must have had
a difficult part to play in acting as host to the heads of the
two opposing parties. In his old age Rich tried to make
amends for his misdeeds by acts of charity, amongst other
benefactions founding and endowing Felsted School in
Essex. It is doubtful, however, if these tardy restitutions
were able to bring comfort to his sordid soul.

In 1577 Wanstead House came into the possession of
the famous Robert Dudley, Earl of Leicester, who in the
May of the following year entertained Queen Elizabeth
there during a visit of five days. A portrait of Her Majesty,
with Wanstead Manor in the background, is still to be seen
at Welbeck Abbey. In November, 1578, Leicester went
through a public form of marriage with the Countess of
Essex, the ceremony having already been privately performed
at Kenilworth. This lady was widow of the murdered Earl
of Essex, and mother of the one who was beheaded. One
of the seats of the Earls of Essex was at Plaistow, within an
easy drive of Wanstead.

At the death of the Earl of Leicester, in 1588, an
inventory was taken of the property, the total value,
including horses, amounting to £1,120. The pictures were
set down as worth £12, and the library no more than

13*s.* 8*d.* This would seem to show that Leicester was not a reading man, and that his pictures, though including portraits of Henry VIII., Mary and Elizabeth, possessed no charms for his contemporaries. Within a year of the Earl's decease, his widow married her third husband, Sir Christopher Blunt.

In 1615 another favourite of royalty, George Villiers, Duke of Buckingham, took Wanstead House, and entertained King James I. there. Four years later Sir Henry Mildmay, one of the judges at the trial of Charles I., came into possession of it. At the Restoration his estate was, of course, escheated, and Charles II. gave it to his brother James, Duke of York. The Duke sold the property to Sir Robert Brooke, who was in residence when Samuel Pepys paid it a visit, on May 14th, 1665. "I took coach to Wanstead," the celebrated diarist writes, "the house where Sir H. Mildmay died, and now Sir Robert Brooke lives there, having bought it of the Duke of York, it being forfeited to him ; a fine seat, but an old-fashioned house, and being not full of people, looks flatly."

In 1667 the estate was bought by Josiah Child, governor —or chairman, as it is now called—of the East India Company. He spent a great deal of money on the grounds, and planted a double row of limes which reached as far as the "Eagle" at Snaresbrook. John Evelyn makes a contemptuous reference to this expenditure in an entry in his diary dated March 16th, 1683. "I went to see," he says, "Sir Josiah Child's prodigious cost in planting walnut trees about his seat, and making fish ponds, many miles in circuit, in a barren spot, as often times these suddenly monied men for the most part seat themselves ; He, from merchant's apprentice and management of the East India Company's stock, being arrived at an estate ('tis said) of £20,000 a year, and lately married his daughter to the eldest son of the Duke of Beaufort, with £50,000 portional present, and various expectations."

Macaulay describes how violently at this time the monopoly of the old East India Company was being attacked. Their profits had been enormous, and their £100 shares were selling for £360. The clamour against the monopoly increased with the accession of William and Mary, but with the vast resources of the Company behind him Sir Josiah fought sturdily on its behalf. It is said that £100,000 was expended in parliamentary bribes, and although the monopoly was declared illegal by the House Sir Josiah's vigorous action kept it still in force. Orders were sent by him to the servants of the Company that no indulgence was to be shown to rival traders. For the ruling of the House of Commons he openly expressed his contempt. "Be guided by my instructions," he wrote to his agents, "and not by the nonsense of a few ignorant country gentlemen who have hardly wit enough to manage their own private affairs, and who know nothing at all about questions of trade." Such a good fighter deserved to win his case, and before his death in 1699 the position of the Company was as strong as it had ever been.

Sir Josiah was succeeded by his son Richard, who became Viscount Castlemaine in 1718, and 1st Earl Tylney in 1732. The title was taken from the Tylney family, a member of which he married. It was the 1st Earl who pulled down the old house in 1715, and built the new one from plans prepared by Sir Colin Campbell. If these plans had been carried out in their entirety, Wanstead House would have been the finest private dwelling-house in Europe. Even in its modified form it was one of the most handsome residences in Great Britain. Built entirely of Portland stone, which becomes whiter with old age, the structure was 260 feet long and 75 feet deep, with a double flight of steps leading to a Corinthian portico. The house cost £100,000, and an equal sum was expended on the grounds, which covered some three hundred acres. Daniel Defoe, in his "Tour through the Eastern Counties," says "Sir Richard Child has laid out the most delicious as well as the most spacious pieces of ground that are to be seen in this part of England."

The 2nd Earl succeeded the 1st Earl in 1750, and was in residence when Horace Walpole visited the house on July 17, 1755. The 2nd Earl had spent large sums of money on art treasures in various parts of Europe. Horace Walpole, himself an ardent collector, was filled with envy at the beautiful bric-a-brac, and relates what a struggle it cost

Photo by J. Adams,   Wanstead Park.   [*Forest Gate.*

[*To face*

him to refuse the many valuable presents his generous host endeavoured to press upon him.

In 1784 the 2nd Earl died without issue, and Sir James Long, a distant relative, inherited the estate, assuming the name of Tylney-Long. At his decease, in 1794, he left an only daughter, Catherine. She was an infant, and during her minority the Prince of Condé, afterwards Louis XVIII., rented the house, till he left it in 1814 to ascend to the throne of France. The young girl was the greatest heiress of the day, being worth at least £80,000 a year. It was only to be expected that, on coming out, she should be surrounded by all the young spendthrifts who were anxious to retrieve their position by marrying a fortune. One of these, the Hon. William Wellesley, son of the Earl of Mornington, and nephew of the great Duke of Wellington, carried off the prize. The bridegroom assumed the name of Pole-Tylney-Long Wellesley on the celebration of the marriage in 1812.

On taking possession of Wanstead House, when the Prince of Condé left it, the young husband set about his task of dissipating the fortune of his wife. His scale of living was almost regal. He kept a pack of staghounds, and a host of hunt servants dressed in Lincoln green. The extravagance of his hunt breakfasts at "The Eagle" at Snaresbrook was the talk of town. No fortune, however magnificent, could stand the strain of such reckless prodigality. In ten years he had spent it all, and to meet his debts was obliged to sell the art curios and furniture of Wanstead House. So numerous were the articles to come under the hammer that the sale lasted thirty-two days, and realised a sum of £41,000. It is interesting to compare this figure with the total of £12 13s. 8d., at which the pictures and library of the old house were valued on the death of the Earl of Leicester in 1588.

A paltry £41,000 was of no service to a man who could not live on £80,000 a year, and the Honourable William was soon in difficulties again. This time the house itself was threatened. No one came forward to make a bid for so princely a structure, and efforts to secure it for the public having failed, one of the most magnificent residences in England was pulled down, merely that the small sum realised by its materials should be divided amongst the creditors. This occurred in 1823, and two years later the once celebrated heiress died of a broken heart, after thirteen years of married life with an almost criminal spendthrift.

His first wife had only been dead three years, when William Wellesley, who, in spite of, or perhaps because of, his reckless character, seems to have been a favourite with the ladies, married Helena, daughter of Colonel Thomas Paterson and widow of Edward Bligh. It took him, of course, very little time to spend her money, and the poor woman was actually compelled to go to the parish for relief, eventually dying in complete destitution. Nothing seemed to affect the spendthrift's health, and in 1842 he became Viscount Wellesley, succeeding to the earldom of Mornington in 1845. The new holder of the title quickly ran through everything that was not in the entail, and then became pensioner of his uncle the Duke of Wellington. How he lived after the Duke's death is not related, but in spite of his dissolute career, he all but reached the Bible limit of threescore years and ten, dying in 1857 at the age of 69.

The earl had no children by his second wife, and the two sons by his first wife died unmarried. His daughter, Lady Victoria Catherine Mary Pole-Tylney-Long Wellesley, did not change her name—she might have felt that it had already been changed sufficiently—and died unmarried as recently as March 30th, 1897. She seems to have come into the property secured by the entail, for being of a charitable disposition, she had the means to build a church at Eastbourne and a convalescent home at Bognor, besides leaving £1000 to the Seamen's Mission. The corporation of the City of London bought the park in 1880 and threw it open to the public in 1882. The pillars of the entrance-gate and the old stables—now the head-quarters of the Wanstead Golf Club, are the sole existing evidences of this once magnificent property.

Only one more word remains to be said about Wanstead House. When it was pulled down in 1823, the Quakers of Plaistow, to which body Mrs. Elizabeth Fry belonged, bought the handsome Corinthian portico, to adorn the entrance to their meeting-house in North Street,

Plaistow. The neighbourhood at that time was full of well-to-do Quakers, and Mr. Curwen says that even in his day he can remember that there were seldom less than twenty carriages waiting on Sunday morning at the meeting-house, while John Bright was often to be seen there. But this branch of the Society of Friends fell on evil days, and had to sell their meeting-house. It was turned into a board school and enlarged, the portico being advanced to the front of the new buildings. The infants of Plaistow, now one of the poorest parishes in the east of London, toddle to their lessons beneath a porchway which once adorned the residence of a king of France, and some eighty years ago was the property of the richest heiress in England. Yet for the most destitute little girl amongst them there can scarcely be in store a harder fate than that which overtook the broken-hearted woman to whom the portico belonged.

CHAPTER IV.

Parsloes—The Fanshawes—Sir Richard Fanshawe, the celebrated Royalist — Lady Fanshawe's Memoirs — Eastbury House — Barking Church—All Saints' Church (West Ham)—Story of West Ham Park—The Cedars—The "Spotted Dog."

ANOTHER old residence, interesting chiefly on account of the family history associated with it, is Parsloes, or Fanshawe's Rookery as it is sometimes called, which lies to the east of Barking and some five or six miles distant from Silvertown. Parsloes figures prominently on every map of Essex which has appeared for the last two hundred and fifty years, down to the latest pocket cycling map of the present day. Yet it is only one of five estates which once belonged to the powerful Fanshawe family.

The Fanshawes originally came from Derbyshire, where they had an estate called Fanshawe Gate. This does not seem to have been a very valuable property, but a younger son, who went to London and became Remembrancer of the Exchequer, made a fortune and bought the Manor of Jenkins near Barking. At his death, in 1568, his nephew, who inherited Fanshawe Gate, also succeeded to the Manor of Jenkins, as well as to the position of Remembrancer of the Exchequer. A little later he added a third estate, Ware Park, in Hertfordshire, to his possessions. By his will he left Fanshawe Gate and Ware Park to his eldest son Henry, Jenkins to his second son Thomas, and sufficient money to his third son William to purchase Parsloes. It was the second son, Thomas, who bought the Manor of Barking for £3,000 from Charles I. in 1628.

It is instructive to note the conflicting statements of the various Essex historians with regard to this single transaction. No less than four of them make a mistake on such an elementary historical point as the dates of the Kings of England. Writing in 1720, Cox says that Sir Thomas

Photo by W. E. Wright.   Parsloes (or Fanshawe's Rookery), near Barking.   [*Forest Gate.*

[*To face*

Fanshaw bought the manor farm from James I. in 1628. James I. had then been dead three years, and Thomas Fanshawe (who spelt his name with an "e") had not yet been knighted. Morant, the acknowledged *doyen* of Essex historians in point of authority, if not in years, repeats the error with regard to the reigning king, but calls the purchaser Thomas Fanshaw, Esq. At length Lysons, in his carefully-written "Environs of London," assigns the right king, Charles I. to the year 1628, but knights the buyer before his time. These varying accounts might well have confused Thomas Wright, who published his history in 1835. In spite of the announcement in his preface that he had taken "great pains to verify all his statements," he declares on one page that James I. sold the manor to Sir Thomas Fanshaw in 1628, and on the next page that Thomas Fanshaw, Esq., bought it in the same year from Charles II. It will be observed that neither of those kings was reigning at that date. Finally "White's Gazetteer," published in 1848 and otherwise trustworthy, persists in the error of putting Charles II. on the throne no less than thirty years before the usually accepted date. The only point on which they all agree is that the amount of the purchase money was £2,000. Yet Patent Roll 4th Charles I., No. 2455, gives £3,000 as the sum.* Surely these writers lend some colour to Sir Robert Walpole's impatient exclamation that "History is a pack of lies."

Sir Thomas Fanshawe's eldest brother, or rather half-brother, Henry, was father of Sir Richard Fanshawe, the celebrated Royalist, and hero of Lady Fanshawe's well-known memoirs. Sir Richard shared the fortunes of the royal family from the outbreak of the civil war to the Restoration, when he was sent as ambassador to Spain and Portugal. In 1844, he married Ann, daughter of Sir John Harrison, and her memoirs give a graphic account of the hardships and perils to which their devotion to the king exposed them. It was not long before Sir Richard was taken prisoner and sent to London. Here, by the kindness of his gaoler he was allowed to meet his wife in a private room at Charing

---

* For most of his information concerning the Fanshawes, the writer is indebted to Mrs. Ridout, daughter of J. G. Fanshawe, Esq., the present owner of Parsloes, and representative of the family.

D

Cross. Lady Fanshawe describes what passed at the interview :

"Then he began to tell how kind his captain was to him, and the people as he passed offered him money, and brought him good things, and particularly Lady Denham at Borstal House, who would have given him all the money she had in her house, but he returned her thanks, and told her he had so ill kept his own that he would not tempt his governor with more, but if she would give him a shirt or two and some handkerchiefs he would keep them as long as he could for her sake. She fetched him two smocks (chemises) of her own and some handkerchiefs, saying she was ashamed to give him them, but having none of her sons at home she desired him to wear them."

This incident would make a pretty subject for a painter of historic scenes. Sir Richard, footsore and travel-stained, has fallen out from the ranks of his dejected fellow-prisoners to snatch a word with Lady Denham, whom he recognises on her balcony. The canvas would represent the cavalier receiving with a courtly bow, amidst the mute astonishment or mocking laughter of the crowd, the linen proffered by his blushing benefactress.

During the whole term of her husband's imprisonment Lady Fanshawe went every morning at four o'clock, on foot and unattended, from her lodgings in Chancery Lane to Whitehall, where he was confined. Standing beneath his window she would call softly to him, "and he, after the first time excepted, never failed to put out his head at the first call. Thus we talked together, and sometimes I was so wet with the rain that it went in at my neck and out at my heels."

Lady Fanshawe accompanied her husband in all his perilous journeys, and the hardships through which they passed may be gathered from the fact that out of twenty children born to them only seven survived their childhood Sir Richard died in his post as ambassador at Madrid in 1666, of an illness brought on by chagrin at being recalled by his ungrateful sovereign.

Of the five original estates Parsloes alone remains to the Fanshawe family. Though only a couple of miles from Barking the quaint old mansion, now uninhabited, seems to lie in the heart of the country. Elizabeth Ogborne, in her History of Essex, published 1814, gives an interesting description of her visit to the house. In the drawing-room, panelled with curiously carved oak, hung a valuable portrait by Vandyke of Sir Richard Fanshawe, and another by the same artist of Sir Simon Fanshawe, who was killed at Naseby. Sir Peter Lely was represented by portraits of Lord and Lady Fanshawe, belonging to the elder branch of the family. The walls are now bare, and in these days of agricultural depression it is to be feared that Parsloes, the sole remaining property of a once powerful Essex family, may be pulled down and the estate parcelled out to separate holders.

Another old manor, of sufficiently artistic design to have found a place in Brayley and Britton's "Beauties of England and Wales," published 1803, and in Virtue's "Picturesque Beauties of Great Britain," published 1834, is Eastbury House, which lies about a mile-and-a-half to the south-east of Barking. The date of its erection is uncertain, but the manor is mentioned as being granted by Henry VIII. to Sir William Denham in 1545. A leaden water-spout at one side of the house bears the date 1573, but Francis Grose in his "Antiquities of England" says that the structure was erected in the reign of King Edward VI. The building consists of a front and two wings, a couple of towers having originally stood in the angles between them. Only one tower remains, the other, it is said, having been destroyed by lightning. The ornamental chimneys are the most conspicuous feature of the house. The roof, which is made of small tiles secured by oak pegs, is still perfectly weather-proof, and the deep red bricks show hardly any signs of decay. In a room which is supposed to have been the chapel, remains of frescoes can be seen upon the walls. The original building had 365 windows, but when the property fell on evil days the majority of them were walled up to evade the window tax.*

* This tax, 5s. per window, was established in 1695 to defray the expense of the recoinage of silver. The effect of its imposition proved most insanitary. To evade it, fan-lights were put in the place of windows above street doors, and light was altogether excluded from the passages and even some of the rooms in the houses of the poor. Although producing a yearly income of over £1,800,000, it was abolished in 1851, and succeeded by the duty on inhabited houses.

Local tradition connects Eastbury House with the Gun-
powder Plot. It is said to have been a meeting-place for
the conspirators, and from its roof they hoped to see the
flames of the explosion which would prove the triumphant
execution of their plot. The usual underground passage is
supposed to connect the house with Barking Abbey, to
which it once belonged. The story probably arose from the
fact that Lord Monteagle resided in the neighbourhood of
Barking. Mr. Tuck, in his "Sketch of Ancient Barking
and Ilford," says that Monteagle's name appears in the
baptismal register of Barking Church.

Prior to the dissolution of monasteries the Vicar of
Barking, who was, of course, a celibate, used to have his
meals, together with his servant, in the convent refectory.
This was found to be an inconvenient arrangement,
"because," as a document of 1536 explains, "the vicar,
being in the execution of his office among his parishioners,
according to his bounden duty in that behalf, could not
always repair to the monastery at the time appointed for
meals or refections, by reason whereof he was often dis-
appointed of his meals; and that it was tedious and
sumptuous for the abbess and convent to cause meats,
drinks, and other substances to be prepared at such extra-
ordinary times and seasons, as they should be driven of
necessity to demand the same." It was therefore agreed
that the vicar should be allowed £10 a year to get his
meals elsewhere. Even allowing for the greater purchasing
power of money at that period, a fraction over sixpence a
day seems but a small sum to provide a vicar and his
servant with both food and drink.

In the churchyard of the parish church there is a monument to Daniel Day, the founder of the old fair at Fairlop
Oak. On the first Friday in July, Day, who seems to have
been a somewhat eccentric character, used to dine beneath
the oak on bacon and beans. Others followed his example,
and presently booths were erected for the sale of various
articles. By 1725 a regular fair was established, William Day
presiding over it and distributing beans and bacon, from
which custom the modern name of "beanfeast" is derived.
Fairlop Oak, whose boughs covered an area of 300 feet in
circumference, was partly burnt by the carelessness of some

Photo by H. E. Wright.]

Eastbury House, near Barking.

[Forest Gate.

[To face

cricketers in 1805, and finally blown down by a gale in 1820.

Barking Church possesses several interesting monuments. In the chancel there is one to Sir Charles Montague, 1625, representing an officer sitting in a tent with two sentinels on guard beside him, and on the chancel floor lie the Tedcastel brasses, dated 1596. Sir Crisp Gascoigne, Lord Mayor of London, who died 1761, has a monument on the wall of the north aisle. He is an ancestor, on the maternal side, of the present Marquis of Salisbury, much of whose property in the neighbourhood is inherited through him. The signature of Captain Cook, the navigator, who married Miss Bates, of Barking, on the 24th of December, 1762, may be seen in the register of marriages.

The old parish church of All Saints, West Ham, which was built in 1181, is the resting-place of a count and two Lord Mayors. The count is John de Bohun, Count of Hereford and Essex, and High Constable of England, who died in 1335. The two Lord Mayors are Sir Thomas Foote (d. 1688) and Sir James Smith (d. 1756). It is difficult to assess the amount of distinction conferred upon a church by sheltering the bones of a deceased Lord Mayor. When it is remembered that the office has been held by at least five hundred persons, and that men of their position would naturally retire to the outskirts of London to end their days, there must be few old suburban churches which cannot boast of at least a brace of them.

George Edwards, the naturalist, and author of " The Natural History of Birds," who died in 1693, was buried in West Ham Church. Here, too, lies one Thomas Cooper, blacksmith, who died in 1768, and whose monument bears the following lugubrious inscription :—

> " My sledge and hammer hath declined,
> My bellows, too, have lost their wind,
> My fire's extinct, my forge decayed,
> And in the dust my vice is laid.
> My coal is spent, my iron's gone,
> My last nail's driven, my work is done."

The story of West Ham Park has been told by Dr. G. Pagenstecher, to whose disinterested exertions the public are indebted for the possession of the property. The earliest house on this estate, of which there is any record, was called Rooke Hall, after its owner. His monument in the parish church tells us little beyond the fact that he had four wives (in due succession, of course) and left £5 a year for bread for the poor. A family named Smyth bought the property in 1666, and sold it nearly a hundred years later to an admiral of the name of Elliot. The cedars which adorn the park are said to have sprung from cones which he brought with him from the cedar trees of the Levant.

In 1762 Dr. Fothergill, a great botanist, became possessed of the estate, and increased its size from thirty to sixty acres. The garden at that time contained a larch, an acacia, and five Virginia cedar trees, but no other foreign plant or shrub. In a few years it became, according to Sir Joseph Banks, the finest garden—with the exception of Kew Gardens—in the whole of Europe. A series of greenhouses 260 ft. in length led out from the house, and contained upwards of three thousand four hundred distinct species of exotic plants. With a view, no doubt, to the future requirements of the navy, Dr. Fothergill laid out a plantation of oak trees with acorns gathered in the mountains of Portugal.

On Dr. Fothergill's death, in 1780, the outlying portions of the estate, including a carriage drive which ran into the Romford Road, were sold, and the name of the house changed from Upton House to Ham House. In 1800 Mr. James Shepherd bought the property, leaving it on his death, twelve years later, to his daughter, who had married Samuel Gurney. This Samuel Gurney was the well-known philanthropist, to whom a monument was erected in Stratford Broadway. He died in 1856, and his eldest son, who lived at Earlham Hall, near Norwich, only survived him by three months. The grandchildren remained in Norfolk, and Ham House was taken by Lady Buxton, Samuel Gurney's sister. It was not till 1866, ten years after the death of the philanthropist, that Overend and Gurney's bank, in which he had been a partner, stopped payment, causing widespread panic and disaster.

Lady Buxton left Ham House in 1868, and four years later, as no new tenant had been forthcoming, John Gurney, Samuel Gurney's grandson, had the building pulled down. Efforts were then made to secure the park for the public, and Mr. Gurney offered it for £25,000, promising to procure £10,000 from his family. A committee was formed to raise the balance of £15,000, but it met with no success, and the estate would doubtless have been sold for building purposes, if Dr. Pagenstecher, who now became secretary to the fund, had not appealed to the coal, corn and finance committee of the City Corporation. It seems that this committee levied taxes on coal and corn for purposes of City improvements, and as they had plenty of money at their disposal, they consented, though West Ham was outside the Metropolitan area, to provide £10,000 if Dr. Pagenstecher would personally guarantee the remaining £5,000. The doctor, who had £4,000 already in hand, gave a personal guarantee for the balance of £1,000. Of this, £300 was collected in the neighbourhood, £300 came from the Society of Friends, and £400 was supplied at a moment's notice by Mr. James Duncan, the generous sugar manufacturer of Silvertown. Thus the full sum was forthcoming and on the 20th of July, 1874, the Lord Mayor, Sir Andrew Lusk, came down in state and opened the park to the public.

Within the confines of the park, but standing in its own grounds, is a house called "The Cedars," formerly known as Upton Lane House, and now the headquarters of the Third Essex Volunteers. This house was built by Mr. Samuel Gurney on the site of an old red-brick mansion, which he had pulled down. Mrs. Elizabeth Fry, his sister, lived here from 1829 to 1844, and here she entertained at lunch on January 31st, 1842, Frederick William IV., King of Prussia, who had met her when at work amongst the inmates of Newgate Prison. From the description which Mrs. Fry gives of the occasion in her diary, the King seems to have enjoyed himself, remarking that it was the best meal he had eaten in England. Before lunch his hostess had introduced him to her brother and sister, eight daughters, seven sons, and 25 grand-children, a ceremony which doubtless contributed to the excellent appetite he displayed.

In Upton Lane, close to the north-east corner of West Ham Park, stands the old inn, called "The Spotted Dog." Here, during the Plague in 1665, it is said that the Stock

Exchange used to meet. The City coat of arms, painted on canvas, still hangs from the wall, though bearing the date of 1603 instead of 1665. Another old building in Upton Lane, scarcely a 100 yards from "The Spotted Dog," is the Red House, now occupied by Major Banes, one of the members for West Ham. There is a report that it was once the residence of General Wolfe. A great friend and fellow officer of his, Sir Hervey Smith, Bart., who was wounded at Quebec, lived and died at West Ham. But there is no evidence that the General himself ever had a residence there, and the name of a certain Jens Woolfe occurring in the title deeds of the Red House, which Mr. Arthur Banes, son of the member, kindly allowed the author to see, may have given rise to the story.

The present vicarage of All Saints Church, standing at the south-east corner of the park, was once a farmhouse, and still possesses a large thatched barn. A thatched cottage in the Portway, a short distance west of the vicarage, is inhabited by Dr. Pagenstecher himself. Apart from its age, the cottage is curious as having been moved bodily some two or three hundred yards to its present position. Nearly opposite the vicarage, the manor of West Ham Burnels, Sir Henry Pelly's residence, used to stand. The carriage drive extended to the present site of St. Mary's Church, Plaistow. Sir Henry gave the ground for the first church, which was built in 1830. With the rapid increase of the surrounding population, the church proved to be too small, and the Rev. S. Given-Wilson, the present vicar, raised funds for a new structure, which was completed about ten years ago. Besides the new church, the vicar has built a children's hospital and two mission churches, his various works in the parish requiring £10,000 a year to maintain.

CHAPTER V.

Plaistow—Dr. Dodd—Dick Turpin—John Wesley—East Ham—
Barking Road—Body-snatching—Smuggling—Prize-fighting.

SEVERAL interesting old buildings still survive in Plaistow.
Cumberland House Farm, which lies to the south of
the northern outfall sewer, and only a mile-and-a-half
from Silvertown, used to belong to Henry, Duke of Cumberland, brother of George III. Here he kept his racing
stud, on account of the excellent pasturage afforded by the
marshes. This duke died in 1790, at the early age of
twenty-four. The house, with its wainscoted walls and
double doors, remains just as it was in the lifetime of its
royal possessor. Still older is the barn in the adjoining
farmyard. It is said to have been a tithes-barn, to which
tenants brought their tithes in corn, and, no doubt,
originally belonged to Stratford Langthorne Abbey. Its
beams are made of horse chestnut, which the wire-worm
will not touch.

Mr. John Spencer Curwen, in his "Old Plaistow," has
given an interesting account of old Plaistow houses, many
of which have been pulled down within the last few years.
In one of these latter resided Dr. Dodd, who was hanged
for forgery towards the close of the eighteenth century.
Dr. Dodd became curate of All Saints Church, West Ham,
in 1751, and renting a house in Plaistow took pupils to
augment his income. Amongst them was Philip Stanhope,
the illegitimate son of the Earl of Chesterfield, and the
recipient of the celebrated letters. An old bootmaker named
Piegrome, who lived in Plaistow, used to show a pattern for
a pair of buckled shoes marked "Honble. Philip Stanhope."

Four of Lord Chesterfield's letters are addressed in 1766
"To Master Philip Stanhope, at Dr. Dodd's house at West
Ham in Essex." In a letter written about this time, he
speaks of Dr. Dodd as "the best and most eloquent

preacher in England, and perhaps the most learned clergyman. He is now publishing notes upon the whole Bible,
as you will see in the advertisements in many of the news-
papers." The noble earl fortunately did not live to see the
learned annotator of the Scriptures die a felon's death upon
the scaffold.

A taste for extravagant living seems to have been the
cause of Dr. Dodd's downfall. In 1766 he took a chapel
in Pimlico as a private speculation, and the fashionable
world soon flocked to hear his sermons. The flatteries of
his wealthy congregation did much to spoil him, and their
society tempted him to live beyond his means. In 1777
his affairs become so embarrassed that he forged a bond for
£4,200 in the name of his late pupil, who had now become
Lord Chesterfield. The forgery was easily detected, and in
spite of the efforts of numerous sympathisers—amongst
them the celebrated Dr. Johnson—and a petition signed by
23,000 persons, the unfortunate clergyman paid the extreme
penalty of the law.

Brunstock Cottage, where Edmund Burke lived from 1759
to 1761, is still to be seen in Balaam Street, Plaistow. Part
of the house was pulled down to make room for a new road,
but the main portion is the same as when the great orator
inhabited it. In Richmond Street stands Richmond House,
once, according to local tradition, the residence of a Duke
of Richmond. The secretary of Jeyes' Sanitary Compound
Company, Ltd., whose manager now inhabits it, has informed the writer that the name of the Duke of Richmond
does not figure in the title deeds, and the present duke
writes to say that he knows nothing of the property. Still,
there is no improbability in a duke possessing a country
house in the same locality where a royal prince was pleased
to keep his racing stud.

In Greengate Street, Plaistow, the walls of a house that
once belonged to the Earls of Essex still stand, a coronet
surmounting the wrought-iron entrance gate. The Earl of
Essex, who was a favourite of Queen Elizabeth, and subsequently beheaded by his fickle sovereign, is said to have
resided here. The house—a large one, containing sixty
bedrooms—was pulled down in 1836, and the present building, which now serves as a lodge to the new Recreation

Photo by] [C. R. Wylie, Esq.

Richmond Street, Plaistow (where Dick Turpin is said to have lived).

[To face p. 42.

Grounds, erected. In the kitchen there is a curiously carved stone mantelpiece, a relic of the original house.

Plaistow in the eighteenth century seems to have been the resort of men who broke the laws and paid the penalty for it, rather than of those who were distinguished for a strict observance of them. Dick Turpin, the famous highwayman, who, like Dr. Dodd, came to a violent end at the hands of the public executioner, figures largely in its annals. Dick Turpin was the son of an innkeeper who owned "The Crown Inn" at Hempstead in Essex, and who combined the trade of butcher with that of retailing beer and spirits. Born in 1705, this son was apprenticed at an early age to a butcher in Whitechapel, from which post, presumably for ill-conduct, he was dismissed. The young man then obtained a situation with a farmer called Giles, who lived in Richmond Street, Plaistow. From this employer Dick Turpin stole two oxen, which were recognised as he was trying to dispose of them at Waltham Abbey Market. Constables were sent to arrest him, but their quarry jumped out of a window and escaped their clutches.

Dick Turpin now became the leader of a gang of smugglers operating between Plaistow and Southend, and made the calling unusually profitable by appropriating the goods of rival smugglers. While engaged in this congenial occupation he married an East Ham girl called Hester Palmer. The district soon became too warm for him, and Turpin withdrew to Epping Forest, where he varied the pastime of stealing deer with daylight housebreaking. While dividing the spoils at an alehouse after an adventure of the latter kind, he and his gang were surprised, but though all his confederates were captured, their leader managed to make good his escape.

Dick Turpin and a man named King now became partners, making a cave in Epping Forest their headquarters. This cave is still pointed out at High Beech, between the Loughton and King's Oak Roads. The two men are said to have lived here six years, Dick Turpin's faithful spouse journeying to and fro to keep them supplied with food. According to popular report there was a certain element of generosity in the highwayman's lawless disposition. Hearing that a widow whom he had robbed was being pressed by her landlord for rent, he threw some gold pieces in at her doorway as he galloped past her house. On another occasion he stopped a country dealer, who had only 15*s.*—all that he was worth—upon his person. Turpin said that he must have the money, but told his victim to take up his stand in Newgate Street at noon the following Monday, with his hat in his hand, and wait to see what would occur. The man did so, and a stranger dropped ten guineas into it.

Thus poor people felt a good deal of sympathy for Dick Turpin, when, in 1737, the Government issued a proclamation offering £200 for his arrest. This proclamation described him as a man "about thirty, by trade a butcher, about 5 ft. 9 in. high, brown complexion, very much marked with the small-pox, his cheek-bones broad, his face thinner towards the bottom, his visage short, pretty upright, and broad about the shoulders." From this description it would appear that the admiration which he excited among the fair sex was more due to the glamour of his deeds than the beauty of his person.

Soon after the proclamation had been issued, Dick Turpin, during one of his rides, fell in with a gentleman mounted on a thoroughbred horse. As his own was a poor one, Turpin invited the stranger to exchange with him. There was no refusing the highwayman's invitation, supported as it was by his usual method of persuasion, and when the gentleman reached home, his mount was found to be a horse which had been stolen from the Plaistow Marshes. A few days later, a London inn-keeper recognised the thoroughbred which Turpin had with him, and tried to arrest its rider. In the scuffle which ensued Dick Turpin accidentally shot his partner King. The notorious highwayman effected his escape, but the loss of his friend, which he seems to have felt a good deal, gave him a distaste for his old haunts, and it was now that he is supposed to have made his celebrated ride to York on Black Bess.

Unfortunately for those who like to cherish this tradition, there is good reason to believe that the description which Harrison Ainsworth gives of the ride in "Rookwood" is solely the offspring of the author's imagination. The story is traceable to an earlier malefactor named Nicks, who, in order to prove an alibi, performed or attempted to perform the ride in 1676. Daniel Defoe refers to the story in his "Tour through Britain."

In Yorkshire Dick Turpin, under the name of Palmer, set up as a horse-dealer, the majority of the horses which he sold having been acquired by his usual methods. He did well in the business, and had excited no suspicion till arrested for shooting a game-cock in a foolish freak. In those days a game-cock which had shown prowess in the pit was a valuable possession, and Dick Turpin was thrown into prison, the inquiries which followed eliciting the fact that many of the horses found in his possession had been stolen from their rightful owners. In this extremity Turpin wrote to his brother at Hempstead, asking for assistance. He neglected, however, to pay the postage, and, his brother refusing to do so, the letter lay at the village post office. Here it caught the eye of the village schoolmaster, who recognised the handwriting. "Thus it was," says Mr. Curwen, to whom the writer is indebted for most of these particulars, "that the Yorkshire people found that their prisoner was the great Turpin." It is not quite clear how this result happened, unless we are to conclude that the schoolmaster opened the letter, learnt where Turpin lay, and at once gave information in order to claim the £200 reward. It is to be hoped, however, that he was not guilty of such treachery towards his former pupil.

Whatever the truth of the story may be, the identity of Palmer the horse-dealer and Dick Turpin the highwayman was satisfactorily established at York. The prisoner was tried at the assizes for horse-stealing and condemned to death, the sentence being carried out on April 7, 1739. An account of the execution says that "Turpin behaved in an undaunted manner: as he mounted the ladder, feeling his right leg tremble he stamped it down, and looking round about him with an unconcerned air he spoke a few words to the topsman (a sporting euphemism for hangman), then threw himself off and expired in five minutes." From this description it seems that in the eighteenth century criminals sentenced to capital punishment were either expected or allowed to be their own executioners, and that it was nothing unusual for their death agonies to be prolonged for at least five minutes.

Association with this notorious law-breaker seems to have blunted for a time the religious sentiment among the people of Plaistow, for they gave but a poor welcome to a very different kind of man who paid them a visit in the same year as Dick Turpin died. This man was John Wesley. In the great preacher's diary, under the date of September 10, 1739, there is the following entry: "I accepted a pressing invitation to go to Plaistow. At five in the evening I expounded there, and at eight again. But most of the hearers were very quiet and unconcerned. In the morning, therefore, I spoke stronger words. But it is only the voice of the Son of God which is able to awake the dead." As John Wesley was riding back to London at the end of his visit he met with an accident. "A person galloping swiftly rode full against me and overthrew both man and horse, but without any hurt to either. Glory be to him who saves both man and beast."

Had the reverend gentleman encountered one of Turpin's late associates, as he fled headlong from justice?

At the beginning of the nineteenth century Plaistow was still a sleepy little village, altogether out of the beaten track and hidden by the lofty elms which grew around it. The Barking Road was not yet built, and the only route from London to Barking lay through Ilford. There was, indeed, a narrow bridge over the Roding at Wall End, called Cow Bridge, but this was only large enough for cattle, and when a trap made use of it one of the wheels had to be taken off. A man at the bridge gatehouse used to charge so much for assisting in the operation.

The upland farms of Plaistow were devoted to potato-growing, while those on the marsh grazed sheep. A local poet of the latter part of the eighteenth century called attention to the fact in the following doggerel lines:

> " Potatoes now are Plaistow's pride,
> Whole markets now are hence supplied.
> Nor finer mutton can you spend,
> Than what our fattening marshes send."

The habitable world ended and the marsh began at Greengate Inn, which still stands at the bottom of Greengate Street. Mr. Curwen thinks that the inn took its name from a green gate, which used to stand opposite to it, and which gave entrance to the marshes. But a writer in the *Essex Review* points out that the original meaning of the Saxon word "gate" or "geat" is the passage itself, and not the obstruction which bars it, so that the "green gate" was more probably a grass-grown entrance to the marshes, than a gate which it was customary to keep painted green. From Greengate Inn the shipping in the Thames could easily be seen, and at high water with good glasses the names of the ships were legible.

A hundred years ago there was only one constable in Plaistow. He wore no uniform, but carried somewhat ostentatiously a pair of pistols, which no doubt had quite as good a moral effect. Very few of the inhabitants possessed a parliamentary vote. In the General Election of 1768 only four persons from Plaistow voted, and they had to go all the way to Chelmsford to do so. London was reached by a daily coach, the fares for which were 3s. return inside and 2s. outside. For this formidable journey of six statute miles the seats had to be booked on the previous night. Another way of getting to London was to walk, and a Plaistow inhabitant who lived to a great age attributed the fact to covering the distance, both ways, on foot for twenty years.

Still more remote from the public highways, if possible, was the village of East Ham. Owing to its proximity to Barking, a good many sailors lived there. Mr. Mathews remembers a man of the name of Ross, who had fought with Lord Cochrane in Chile, and taken part in the cutting out of the frigate "Esmeralda." The village used also to suffer from the raids of the press gangs, who would steal up from Barking Creek at night in search of prey. On one occasion the young men of Barking and East Ham combined against a gang, and after overpowering the men, deprived the officer of his sword. The ringleaders were subsequently captured and taken before Lord Ellenborough. They would probably have been transported for life if the officer, whom they had refrained from ill-treating, had not interceded for them.

In 1807 the remote little villages of Plaistow and East Ham were roused from their sleep of many centuries' duration by the commencement of the making of the Barking Road. The East India Docks, which lie on the Middlesex side of Bow Creek, had no means of communication with the Essex side, except by a wide *détour* across Bow Bridge. The dock company decided to build a new road, which would give facilities for goods from Essex intended for their docks, and also provide a shorter route from Barking— where all the fish for London were landed—to the metropolis. An iron bridge was thrown across Bow Creek close to the eastern end of the Docks, and an almost straight road built to Barking along a line which separated the uplands of Plaistow and East Ham from the marshy levels to the south of them.

The road, which was completed in 1810, did not at first realise the expectations formed of it. Being built for the most part on marshy ground, it became very rotten, and heavy traffic avoided it. The driver of the Barking coach used to send his team along the paths on either side of it. Several years elapsed before the man at the toll gate on the Iron Bridge took enough money to pay his own wages. The foot passengers were nearly all of the poorest class, and the toll-keeper was often driven to accept a pocket-knife in pawn, owing to the unavoidable absence of the regulation halfpenny. As late as 1845, there were only six houses between Plaistow and the Iron Bridge.

The Barking Road did not at once bring full enlightenment to the old-world villages of Plaistow and East Ham, and body-snatching survived its advent a good many years. A regular gang existed at Barking, and whenever a burial took place at East Ham Church the grave had to be watched at night till nature had rendered the corpse valueless for sale. In 1834 Mr. Mathews remembers a man, from the shelter of the church porch, watching over the grave of a relative, in company with two or three friends and a large sheep dog. When a couple of body-snatchers made their appearance, the dog gave chase and held one of them till the watchers came up and secured him. The capture of the other was also effected, and they each got two months' imprisonment.

Smuggling also continued to flourish in the neighbourhood, though this was winked at, if not actually encouraged,

Photo by J. Adams,]

[Forest Gate.

The "Spotted Dog," Upton.

by the inhabitants, who got their luxuries cheap on account of it. Smacks used to bring tobacco and spirits up Barking Creek, and land them on the marshes. The goods were taken away in deep-bodied carts fitted with false bottoms. The residents were well acquainted with the smugglers, and were careful to avoid betraying them. Occasionally, as the smugglers passed a cottage in the dark of night, its owner, standing at the door, would say in a low voice, " Drop us a keg." And the keg would be dropped, to make certain of the speaker's friendliness.

A locality of this kind, close to London, and yet far from the beaten track, was just the neighbourhood for prize fights, and in the fall of the year, Mr. Mathews says, hardly a week passed without an encounter. A ring would be made in the marshes just below East Ham Church, and some sixty or seventy flies and dog-carts would come down from town. The practice survived till 1840, when East Ham was provided with modern police. The last fight took place in November of that year. A thick fog came on during the afternoon, and when the traps tried to find their way back to town, numbers of them drove into a pond which lay on the wayside between the church and the "White Horse" Inn. Cart horses had to be sent for to extricate the heavier ones from the mud into which the wheels had sunk.

The ill name for fever and ague which marshes possess, no doubt retarded the growth of the southern portions of East and West Ham. Cooke, in his " Modern British Traveller" published 1802-1810, says that the climate of Essex is "particularly unhealthy" on that account. In a book called "The Professional Excursions of an Auctioneer," published 1843, the author speaks of the "proverbial insalubrity" of the climate, and remarks that "the citizen trembles at the name of the marshes"; on the other hand, if living to old age is a proof of good health, the district should be salubrious enough. Lysons notices that the ages recorded in East Ham Churchyard are unusually high, and Mrs. Ireland, who had an estate in Plaistow on the edge of the marsh, attained to her hundredth year. The Rev. R. W. B. Marsh, late vicar of St. Mary's, Plaistow, says he has buried five centenarians, and tells a story of an old woman

E

who was one of his parishioners. When visiting her one day, the old woman said, "I cannot tell what's the matter with my daughter there; she sits in her chair, and I can hardly move her to help me in the housework." The daughter was eighty years of age, the mother one hundred and two.

The poorer inhabitants of the district retained their unsophisticated character to comparatively recent times. When the Great Exhibition was opened in 1851, nearly all employers of labour sent their hands to see it. Mr. Mathews' brother took up one day about eighty of his father's farm labourers, all dressed in their white smocks. On entering the Exhibition, so as to keep together, they were told to walk two and two. A fine labourer, called Cabal, headed the procession, crying as he went: "Hoorah, lads, make room for the governor!" When they reached the head of the building Cabal took off his hat and, wiping the perspiration, said, "If this ain't wuss nor diggin' o' taturs!"

Such was Cabal's judgment on this wonderful display of the latest triumphs of civilisation.

CHAPTER VI.

Maryland Point—North Woolwich—The Devil's House—Kent in Essex—Ham Creek—River Ferries—"Prince Regent's" Public-house.

WEST HAM, like East Ham and Plaistow, was only a small village at the beginning of the 19th century. Old Bow Bridge still stood. It had been repaired from time to time, but was practically the same structure which Queen Maud had built seven centuries earlier. The new bridge did not replace it till 1839. Stratford, according to David Hughson's "London," published 1806, was full of pleasant suburban residences belonging to rich citizens, some five or six hundred carriages being kept in the neighbourhood. Maryland Point, so named by a merchant who had made his money in Maryland, contained several handsome houses. "In the memory of man," remarks Salmon, the Essex historian, writing in 1760, "it was a rabbit warren." Forest Gate was not known by that name, Woodgrange and Upton comprising the whole of it. A toll-gate, from which the locality afterwards took its name, stood at the entrance to Wanstead Flats.

As for Silvertown and North Woolwich, they did not come into existence till many years later than 1800. At that date only one house was to be seen in the wide expanse of marsh between Bow Creek and Barking Creek. This was called the Devil's House, and stood on the banks of Gallion Reach, a little to the east of the present entrance to the Albert Docks. There are many conflicting explanations of the origin of its name. Some think that "Devil's House" is a corruption of "Duval's House," a Dutchman, whom they suppose to have built it. Mr. Henry Carter, Marsh Bailiff to the borough of West Ham, spells the name "Deval," and Mr. Mathews, De Wall. Others have confused the name with that of Claude Duval, the celebrated

E 2

highwayman, and imagine the house to have been his residence. There is no authority, however, for believing that he ever lived in the neighbourhood.

Mr. W. T. Vincent, in his "Records of the Woolwich District," says that he has traced the "Devil's House" as far back as 1720. Although Cox, the Essex historian of that date, makes no mention of it in his books, nor marks it on his map, Peter Muilman in 1770 speaks of it by that name. In 1802, a publication called "The Water Companion from Gravesend to London," mentions the "Devil's House" as the only landmark on the northern bank between Bow Creek and Barking Creek, and goes on to say, "The Devil's House was once a public-house, and is probably so called in derision from being part of a religious order, for the Monastery of Stratford Langthorne was possessed of lands in this part of Woolwich."

Although the explanation here given is not satisfactory in itself, it seems to afford a clue to one. In a history of Kent by John Harris, published in 1719, the author says, when speaking of Woolwich, "This parish hath 500 acres of land and some few houses (saith an old manuscript which I have seen) on the Essex side of the Thames; and there was also a chapel-of-ease." In 1770, Muilman repeats the story about the chapel-of-ease, "the foundations of which," he says, "are still visible. The houses are all fallen down, except the 'Devil's House,' an alehouse near Thames Wall, much frequented in summer time." At one period it is probable that the ruined chapel-of-ease and the public-house were the only two buildings visible on the bank of the river opposite Woolwich. The contrast between the purposes for which they had each been erected would strike the most casual observer. According to the old lines :

> "Wherever God erects a house of prayer,
> The devil's sure to build a chapel there."

This couplet may very probably have given rise to the title of the "Devil's House."

At the beginning of the nineteenth century the "Devil's House," together with the land attached, some hundred and thirty acres, was occupied by the Ismay French family. In later years it became a mere shelter for marshmen, who tended cattle on the marshes. Walter White, in his "Eastern England," published 1865, mentions the "Devil's House" as a "building with a red roof, standing all alone in the midst of the pastures," in which hundreds of Scotch cattle grazed. The house was finally bought by the Albert Dock Company, who pulled it down on making the Dock entrance, close to which it stood.

"More wealth passes through Woolwich than any place in the world" is an old saying, explained by the fact that the parish of Woolwich is to be found on both sides of the Thames. The question why a part of Kent should lie on the north side of the river has engaged the attention of each Essex historian in turn, without eliciting a satisfactory explanation from any one of them. The distribution of West Ham, East Ham and Kent on the north bank of the river is somewhat curious. West Ham extends from Bow Creek to the West Ham Sewage Pumping Station, on the site of old Ham Creek. From the pumping station to the Nucoline Works comes a narrow strip of East Ham, followed by a patch of Kent extending to the North Woolwich Gardens. These Gardens, which from their name might be supposed to belong to Woolwich, are a portion of East Ham, and then comes another patch of Kent reaching to a line which bisects the Northern Outfall Sewage Works. From this line to Barking Creek lies a portion of Barking district.

Wright and some other Essex historians, in order to account for the presence of Kent in Essex, say that the river changed its course, cutting off a piece of Kent and leaving it on the northern bank. Perhaps this is the most foolish explanation of any, for the northern river banks still stand as the Romans made them, and it is inconceivable that the Thames should suddenly have changed its course, so as to leave a portion of its southern bank intact upon its northern bank. Others say that the reason is to be found in connection with the bodies of drowned persons washed ashore on the Essex bank. East Ham village being two miles distant refused to move in the matter, and the duty of burying them fell upon the inhabitants of Woolwich, who received in compensation 500 acres on the northern river bank.

This explanation, though plausible enough, is supported by no evidence, and a more satisfactory reason has to be found. It is hardly necessary to go back, like a writer in the *Essex Review*, to the Roman period, when the Iceni, who held the country on both sides of the river, were defeated to the north of it and only managed to retain the strip of marshland on that bank. It will be sufficient to refer to the origin of the present English counties.

The writer of the article "County" in the "Encyclopædia Britannica" says that it is an error to suppose that Alfred the Great, or any other king, divided England up into an arbitrary number of hundreds and counties. The counties, hundreds, townships, down to even the parishes and manors, are all traceable to independent tribal settlements amongst the early Saxons. The voluntary combination of these parishes and townships would make a hundred, and a combination of hundreds formed the county. If, then, a lord of the manor on one side of a river happened to possess land on the other side, this land would be included in the county in which the manor was finally merged. In the present case, according to Hasted's "History of Kent," published 1778, Count Haimo, Vicecomes or Sheriff of Kent in William the Conqueror's reign, had land on both sides of the river at Woolwich, and in this way the property on the north bank became included in the county of Kent.

Some authorities are inclined to doubt that a Chapel of Ease ever stood at North Woolwich, contending that there would be no need for a chapel in the midst of uninhabited marshland. But the river bank at this part was not always destitute of houses, for Lysons mentions a flood in 1236 which drowned a number of persons and cattle on the north side of the river. The recurrence of these floods, caused by breaches in the river wall, made North Woolwich uninhabitable, and resulted in the desertion of the houses and the chapel. The last flood of which there is any record occurred in the reign of James I. Any doubts as to the existence of the chapel are removed by the fact that, as Mr. Carter points out, there still exists at North Woolwich an old water-course called Chapel Fields Sewer, and some meadows called Chapel Fields.

After the flood in the reign of James I., the next histori-

Photo by]

IC. R. Wylie, Esq.

Cable Steamship "Silvertown," at Passage, Queenstown.

[To face p. 54.

cal reference to the district, Mr. Vincent says, is to be found in the year 1656, when Ham Creek was let by its owner to Cromwell for the use of the English navy. Ham Creek, which no longer exists, used to run up from the present pumping station almost as far as Greenstreet House, and formed the boundary between East and West Ham. Charles II. ratified the agreement which Cromwell had made, and Captain Badeley, of the King's Dockyard, Woolwich, applied to him for orders to remove the guns and ballast from the *Success*, and haul her into Ham Creek. The Silvertown Roman Catholic Church stands over the old channel of the creek, with one half in West Ham and the other half in East Ham.

During the war against the Dutch in 1667, Sir Allan Apsley was stationed with a regiment at North Woolwich. In a letter, dated "The Marsh over against Woolwich, July 17th, 1667," he complains of the locality on account of the fever and ague, and says that his men "cannot be persuaded that they are obliged to stay." It was probably on this occasion that the Government acquired their land at North Woolwich. Although no barracks were built, a portion of the ground appears to have been used to store old ordnance. Major Murdock, late of the Ordnance Store Department, Woolwich, thinks that this old ordnance was landed at North Woolwich about the same time that 1,200 tons of old guns and iron were sent to be melted down for the pillars of old Westminster Bridge. In 1777, according to Mr. Mathews, a detachment of soldiers was engaged in repairing Manor Way—which was a military road belonging to the Government—with material supplied by the old stone cannon lying at North Woolwich.

The right to ply a ferry between Woolwich and the Essex side was an ancient privilege, which is first mentioned as far back as 1308. At the beginning of the nineteenth century a horse ferry was in use, capable of taking a horse and trap, or the cattle which Kent farmers sent to the Romford market. The man who worked the ferry lived in an old barge, dragged up the shore above high-water mark. This barge was subsequently replaced by an inn on the river bank, called after it "The Old Barge Inn."

In 1811 a rival horse ferry was established higher up the

river, between Old Charlton and Plaistow Level. Its object
was, probably, to enable the inhabitants of Woolwich and
Charlton to take advantage of the improved means of communication afforded by the Barking Road, which had been
completed the previous year. A road connecting the ferry
with the Barking Road was built across the marshes and
called Prince Regent's Lane. It joined the Barking Road
at the old "Greengate Inn" at Plaistow.

A ferry is never considered complete without an inn at
each landing-place, and in 1812 the "Marquess of Wellington" was built on the Charlton side. It will be remembered that this was the year in which the Earl of Wellington
—his title at that time—was created Marquis of Wellington
for his victories in the Peninsula. The inn stood at a spot
near the centre of Messrs. Siemens' present works. On the
Plaistow side arose "Prince Regent's" public-house, the
site of which was close to where Prince Regent's Wharf,
belonging to Messrs. Burt, Boulton and Haywood, Ltd.,
now stands. The "Prince Regent's" public-house —named,
like the lane, after the Prince who was created Regent in
1811—was much frequented by sportsmen who went to
Plaistow marshes for the shooting. In later years the inn
became a favourite resort for moonlight boating parties.

The "Prince Regent" public-house existed till 1847,
when the North Woolwich Railway was built, and the railway steam ferry-boats took away the custom from the
Charlton ferry. It was then pulled down, and another
house, bearing the same name, erected higher up Prince
Regent's Lane, on the spot now occupied by the "Prince
of Wales" public-house. With the second "Prince Regent"
public-house is associated the name of Byron Noël, Viscount
Ockham. According to an obituary notice which appeared
in the *Daily Telegraph* on September 6, 1862, the story of
this Viscount Ockham was a curious one. He was the
eldest son of the Right Hon. William, 8th Lord King,
raised to the Earldom of Lovelace at the coronation of
the Queen in 1838. Viscount Ockham's mother was, in
the grandiloquent phraseology of the *Daily Telegraph*, of
the early sixties, "a lady of hereditary interest far beyond
that narrow pale of the peerage roll, as the only child
of Lord Byron and the Ada of his poems." The viscount's

grandmother was the heiress of the Noëls, "the amiable and ill-starred wife of the proud and haughty poet-lord."

Viscount Ockham entered the Navy as a middy, but left it after a few months' service. "Pride of soul," says the *Daily Telegraph,* "would not allow him to obey his superiors." It allowed him, however, to serve as a sailor on an American merchant ship, and on his return to England to work as a common labourer in Mr. Scott Russell's ship-building yard in the Isle of Dogs. While employed here, he used to spend most of his spare time at the "Prince Regent's" public-house. He is said to have married a woman belonging to the class amongst whom he lived. If so, when, on the death of his grandmother in 1860, he succeeded to the Barony of Wentworth, this woman could have claimed the right to be presented at Court. The claim was never made, for Viscount Ockham's tastes lay more with the bar of the "Prince Regent's" public-house than with the drawing-room of Buckingham Palace. He died of the rupture of a blood-vessel, at the early age of twenty-six.

The old "Prince Regent's" public-house, the old "Barge House," and the "Devil's House" were the only three buildings on the river front between Bow Creek and Barking Creek from 1811 to 1828. In the latter year a philanthropist named Mills built, at a cost of £10,000, a settlement at North Woolwich. It consisted of a large private house, occupied by himself, and ten small cottages. His purpose was to give employment to London waifs and strays, and brick-making was the work he chose. The undertaking proved a failure, either because there was no clay suitable for brickmaking, or because of the difficulties of transport when the bricks were made. The houses were vacated and fell into decay, a process accelerated by visitors from East Ham, who took away whatever they could carry. George Durrant, a boatman in the employ of the India-rubber, Gutta-percha, and Telegraph Works Company, Limited, remembers bathing as a boy close to this deserted settlement, and afterwards inspecting Mr. Mills' house, which was a handsome building, with beautiful paintings on the walls.

CHAPTER VII.

Eastern Counties Railway — North Woolwich Railway — North Woolwich Gardens—C. J. Mare's Shipbuilding Yard—Messrs. Silver & Co.—Victoria Docks.

A NEW era now began to dawn over the district of West Ham, heralding changes which are perhaps unequalled in the history of any other portion of the United Kingdom. The Eastern Counties Railway was incorporated in 1836, and in 1839 the first section from Devonshire Street to Romford was opened. Great things were expected of it, 22 per cent. being the lowest estimate of the dividends it was to pay. At the inauguration banquet, one of the speakers, Mr. Thomas Evans, said that if he lived to see the completion of this and similar undertakings, he believed that he would live to see "misery almost banished from the earth." Mr. Evans was not the first man to think that a new industrial method, or some fresh discovery of science, was destined to revolutionise the world. As a writer has already put it, De Quincey when opium relieved his toothache felt that the drug would prove the salvation of mankind. Bliss would be sold by the gallon, and distributed by coaches to the remotest corners of the land. Opium has now been known to the country for many years, but the millennium is no nearer than before its introduction.

As early as 1833 notice had been given of a Parliamentary Bill to form a railway "from Commercial Road, Limehouse, to the River Thames at East Ham, opposite Woolwich." It was not, however, till 1846, that a railway from Stratford Market to North Woolwich was actually commenced. The object of the line was to tap the traffic from South Woolwich. The railway from London Bridge to Greenwich—the first one out of London—had been built in 1838, but the expensive tunnelling required to carry it on to Woolwich delayed its extension for several years to come. This gave the opportunity for the construction of a rival route to Woolwich across the level marshland on the north bank of the river.

For the promotion of this railway, Messrs. Kennard, Brassey and Peto were associated. They were soon joined by Bidder. Brassey, the father of the present Lord Brassey, had worked his way up from a labouring man to a position amongst the foremost contractors of the day. George Bidder was the celebrated "calculating boy." He had been picked up in the country by Robert Stephenson, who came across him in the execution of one of his engineering works. Bidder was self-educated, having learnt figures with the use of beans. He could do the most complicated calculations by means of his self-taught methods.

Bidder, besides being a clever engineer, possessed a far-seeing capacity for business, and it was at his suggestion that his associates bought the whole of the land from Bow Creek to Gallion's Reach, and from Barking Road to the River Thames. This area includes the ground now covered by the Victoria and Albert Docks, as well as the river frontage occupied by numerous thriving factories. At that time, the property, mere marshland, with only three houses on the whole extent of it, was to be had for two figures an acre. At the present day, an acre on the river front cannot be bought for less than four or five thousand pounds.

The railway to North Woolwich was opened in June, 1847; two steam ferries having been built to connect it with South Woolwich. Barking Road was the only station from Stratford Market to the terminus. It stood on the site of the old Canning Town Station, on the Woolwich side of the Barking Road. After leaving Barking Road the railway followed the course of the present goods line by the side of the North Woolwich Road, the route *viâ* Tidal Basin and Customs House not being built till the Victoria Docks were made in 1855. From Barking Road to North Woolwich the railway ran through uninhabited marshland, in which, with the exception of Prince Regent's Lane, no roads of any description existed. At North Woolwich a row of cottages for those employed on the railway sprang up, but in 1848, according to White's "Essex Gazetteer" of that date, the

North Woolwich stationmaster was still residing in East Ham.

The extension of the South-Eastern Railway from Greenwich to South Woolwich took place in 1849, and the North Woolwich Railway thus lost the major portion of its traffic. The Land Company tried to attract inhabitants to the district by offering cheap season-tickets on the railway—which they controlled—to all who rented houses on their property. For £2 10s. a householder could obtain a first-class season-ticket to Shoreditch for the whole year. The price is now £10.

A season-ticket is, after all, but a small bait to tempt a man to live in malarious swamp, and a member of the Land Company—in all probability the resourceful Bidder —hit upon the idea of attracting passengers by creating an East End rival to Cremorne at North Woolwich. The North Woolwich Gardens were commenced in 1849, being laid out with great care by skilful landscape-gardeners. The bowling-greens were said to have been exceptionally fine. The opening ceremony took place in May, 1851, the same month as that of the Great Exhibition. Although the latter could hardly be said to have suffered from the rivalry, there is no doubt that many East Enders who could not afford to see the Exhibition consoled themselves with the less magnificent, but at the same time less expensive, delights of the North Woolwich Gardens.

Unfortunately, as time went on, the North Woolwich Gardens acquired the same undesirable reputation as Cremorne Gardens, and a movement was set on foot amongst influential landowners in the district to do away with their dancing and drinking licence, and make them public property. For this purpose a fund was started and a committee formed, under the presidency of the Duke of Westminster and with Mr. S. B. Boulton (of Burt, Boulton and Haywood, Ltd.) as one of the vice-chairmen. Amongst others who took an active part in the matter were the Bishop of St. Albans, Canon Proctor, and Sir Spencer Maryon Wilson. The required sum, £20,000 (or £2,000 an acre), was collected, and the Gardens were thrown open to the public in 1890. They are now under the control of the London County Council.

Photo by]   [C. R. Wylie, Esq.

About to let go Buoy off s.s. "Silvertown."

[To face p. 60

The first firm to take advantage of the new railway, and settle on the river bank between Bow Creek and Barking Creek, was C. J. Mare's shipbuilding business, from which the present Thames Ironworks and Shipbuilding Co., Ltd., has sprung. C. J. Mare had been partner in the firm of Ditchburn & Mare, which migrated from Deptford and set up on the Blackwall side of Bow Creek in 1836. Mr. George Colby Mackrow, naval architect to the Thames Ironworks, signed articles to learn "the art and mystery of shipbuilding" with Ditchburn & Mare in 1844, and has served with practically the same firm for 56 years. The writer is indebted for his information on the subject to an account which Mr. Mackrow has published in the *Thames Ironworks Quarterly Gazette.*

In 1844 Messrs. Ditchburn & Mare occupied small premises in Orchard Yard, where the present offices of the Thames Ironworks stand. Orchard Yard was named after "Orchard House," an old inn on the Blackwall side of the creek, celebrated for its orchard, which was in full bloom when Mr. Mackrow joined the firm. Orchard House figures in old maps as the extreme limit of the eastern outskirts of London. Even in 1844 it was still called Land's End, and Mr. Mackrow's family, who lived in Stepney, considered that he had gone to work in the wilds of the country. At "Orchard House" Inn passengers used to embark upon the adventurous voyage to Gravesend, and the primitive character of the spot was emphasised by the fresh shrimps which were landed every morning. There was an uninterrupted view across Bow Common as far as the Mile End Road.

Mr. Charles John Mare or "Charlie" Mare, as he was familiarly, though not disrespectfully, called by his workmen, came of a good Cheshire family, succeeding, on his father's death, to the Manor of Hatherton and Shavington-cum-Gristy. He leased his ancestral home in order to find the purchase money for his partnership with Ditchburn. Although not trained to business, he showed considerable aptitude for it, and in 1846 suggested to his partner that, in view of the excessively high railway tariff for conveying iron from the north, they should buy some land on the Essex side of the creek, and lay down plant for rolling their own iron. Mr. Ditchburn was opposed to the idea, and the partnership came to an end.

Mr. Mare at once took four acres on the opposite side of the creek, and set up for himself. At that time the four acres were covered with reeds, and submerged at spring tides. But the ground was soon cleared, offices and workshops erected, and two slips laid down. From these Mr. Mare launched eight above-bridge steamers in succession. His workshops were next busy constructing the celebrated Menai Tubular Bridge, and then he obtained the contract for the new Westminster Bridge, over which he lost heavily. In 1856, owing to the low figure at which he had agreed to build some fifteen gunboats and despatch vessels for the Crimean War, Mr. Mare became insolvent, and his works were taken over by the Thames Ironworks and Shipbuilding Company, Ltd.

In 1858 the new company received an order from the Admiralty for H.M.S. "Warrior," the first sea-going ironclad ever built. The idea was taken from a suggestion of Napoleon III. to plate two floating batteries with $3\frac{1}{2}$-in. armour to attack the forts at Kilburn in the Crimea. The "Warrior," which was launched in 1860, was regarded as a great innovation by the Admiralty, who had a prejudice against iron ships. After the trial, which was very satisfactory, Sir John Pakington, First Lord of the Admiralty, said to Mr. Rolt, chairman of the company, "I often wonder how I mustered sufficient courage to order the construction of such a novel vessel."

That the "Warrior" was thoroughly successful in every way is shown by the fact that, after forty years' service, she was only struck off the active list on the 10th of March, 1900, when her original engines were still in use. Since its formation the Thames Ironworks, which now cover thirty acres of ground on the Essex side, have turned out more than 830 vessels, besides other works, amongst which may be mentioned Blackfriars Bridge, Hammersmith Bridge, the roof of the Westminster Aquarium, and the pontoons for the Woolwich Free Ferry.

After his failure in 1856, Mr. Mare promoted a company called the Millwall Iron and Shipbuilding Works, erecting an armour-plate rolling mill at the cost of £100,000. The firm secured one or two good orders, but soon became insolvent, the price of coal on the Thames preventing them from competing successfully with ironworks in the North. Mr. Mare made several attempts to rehabilitate his fortunes, but without success. In 1848 he had married the daughter of Peter Rolt, a rich timber merchant and member of Parliament for Greenwich, who, after his son-in-law's failure, formed the company to carry on the business. The daughter had been presented at Court, and was one of the beauties of the season. In 1852 Mr. Mare represented Plymouth in the Conservative interest, and became a great friend of Disraeli, with whom he was often to be seen walking on the parade at Brighton. Mr. Mackrow, who knew him well, says that he was a most abstemious man, seldom taking wine and never smoking. He enjoyed the best of spirits, made friends everywhere, and was beloved by all.

There is a sad sequel to the story. The founder of one of the largest engineering works in Great Britain, the representative of a wealthy seaport, and the friend of England's most powerful minister, died in absolute poverty at Limehouse as recently as February, 1898. The only tribute to his memory were a few poor ears of corn, which his widow, the Court beauty of former days, placed in his coffin. He had plucked them for her more than half a century before.

No other firm joined the shipbuilding yard on the river front, between Bow Creek and Barking Creek, till 1851, when two brothers named Howard bought a couple of acres in the centre of the property, which now belongs to the India-rubber, Gutta-percha, and Telegraph Works Co., Limited. On these two acres they built a glass factory and a wharf, at which to load schooners with the goods they manufactured. In 1852, S. W. Silver and Co., the well-known outfitters in Cornhill, removed their waterproofing works from Greenwich to some land adjacent to Howard's factory. The first purchase was a single acre, but five more were soon added, and when the Howards shortly failed, the two acres belonging to them were also secured. There were still no roads, and the only way to reach the works was by the river wall from North Woolwich or Barking Road.

In 1855 a great change came over the neighbourhood, by

the opening of the Victoria Docks. They extended from their entrance near Bow Creek to within half a mile of S. W. Silver's Works. At the same time the loop line to the north of the Docks was made, and stations built at Tidal Basin and Custom House. The old line, for which a Swing Bridge was erected across the Dock entrance, remained in use for goods traffic only.

As soon as the Docks were opened, William Cory & Son, coal merchants, acquired their coaling station within the docks, and close to the entrance. This firm's success in cheapening seaborne coal made it possible for Silvertown factories to contend successfully against their favoured rivals in the north. Before this time seaborne coal had been carried in brigs, unloaded by "whipping" in the "Pool" below London Bridge. "Whipping" was a purely manual operation. A basket was lowered into the brig by a rope running over a pulley. When full, it was hauled up by the weight of two or three men jumping off a raised staging.

The process was a slow one, and in the case of the screw colliers which began to supersede the brigs required too many men to be remunerative. Accordingly, Mr. William Cory, as soon as he had established himself in the Docks, ordered a set of hydraulic cranes from Sir William Armstrong's works. By this means he was able to reduce the price of seaborne coal to 7s. 6d. per ton, while the railborne coal remained at 12s. 6d. per ton. The men were paid according to the time they took to unload a steamer, and £2 15s. a week was not at all an unusual sum for them to earn.

Not content with the advantages gained by the introduction of hydraulic cranes, Mr. Cory conceived the idea of a floating wharf anchored in the river, where he would have to pay no dock dues, and alongside of which colliers could be brought at any state of the tide. In 1859 the Thames Ironworks had made, from the plans of an American, a large floating derrick, designed for raising sunken vessels. It may not be generally known that a derrick, which is a contrivance for raising heavy weights, was so called from its resemblance to a gallows invented by Derrick, a celebrated hangman at the beginning of the seventeenth century, by which the victims were hanged by being hoisted into the air, instead of, as at present, being dropped from a platform towards the ground.

The floating derrick in question, some 270 ft. long and 90 ft. wide, was divided into a number of watertight compartments and furnished with a powerful steam crane. Though proved to be a failure for the work for which it was designed, it suited Mr. Cory's purpose admirably. Engines and cranes were put on board by Sir William Armstrong's firm, a workshop where all necessary repairs could be effected was fitted up, and gas for lighting was manufactured on the vessel itself.

CHAPTER VIII.

Charles Dickens' "Londoners Over the Border"—The Rev. H.
Douglas—St. Mark's Church, Victoria Docks.

MEANWHILE the population of the district was increasing
rapidly, and a description of the immediate neighbourhood of the Victoria Docks, written by Charles
Dickens himself, appeared in *Household Words* for September 12th, 1857, in a paper entitled "Londoners Over
the Border." The "Border" is the River Lea, London
proper coming to an end with Middlesex, on the west
bank, and Essex beginning on the east bank. The article
commences :

"There is a suburb on the border of the Essex marshes
which is quite cut off from the comforts of the Metropolitan
Buildings Act ; in fact, it lies just without its boundaries,
and therefore is chosen as a place of refuge for offensive
trade establishments turned out of town ; those of the oil-
boilers, gut-spinners, varnish-makers, printers' ink-makers,
and the like. Cut off from the support of the Local
Managing Act, this outskirt is free to possess new streets
of houses without drains, roads, gas or pavement."

The paper goes on to say that the suburb consists of
two new towns, Hallsville, "called into existence in 1847
by Mare & Co.'s ship-building yard, and half depopulated
by the recent bankruptcy of that firm ;" and Canning Town,
created by works in progress at the Victoria Docks. Both
towns are adjacent to the Barking Road Station of the
Eastern Counties Line. The view from this station in
summer is inviting. The broad green Essex plain is
master of the situation. Cattle graze on the green grass,
and belts of trees with the spire of a distant church are
seen on the horizon. On a closer inspection, however, the
settlement is far from bearing out the agreeable promise of

Photo by]   Lowering Steam Launch from s.s. "Silvertown."   [C. K. Wylie, Esq.

To face p. 66.

the landscape. The houses are run up at the cost of only £80, and are mere band-boxes placed on the top of the ground. The ditches at the back of them are nothing more or less than cesspools. The area in this district covered by dikes alone amounts to 140 acres.

The surface of the country lies 7 ft. below high-water mark, with the result that in winter the roads become impassable. The doctor of the place is driven to wearing sea boots, and the clergyman, whose name, appropriately enough, is Marsh,* loses his shoes through neglecting to take a similar precaution. The national school is a wooden lean-to, where the mistress, when it rains, conducts the lessons beneath her umbrella, to protect herself from the leaking roof. Only the poorer class of unskilled labourers live here. The well-paid mechanics reside in Stratford or Plaistow. Fever and ague abound, and once when Hallsville had the same population as Plaistow, there were, for the same period of time, only sixteen deaths in the latter, compared with seventy-two deaths in the former.

When due allowance is made for Dickens' habitual tendency towards exaggeration, this account is found to be substantially correct. The only drains were the marsh dikes, which being cut off from the river by the Victoria Docks no longer possessed an outflow. Although the inhabitants paid a highway rate, the roads, having their foundations in the marsh, could not be kept in proper repair.

The article by Charles Dickens received confirmation from the Rev. H. Douglas, who in 1857 was appointed by Dr. Tait, then Bishop of London, to be resident clergyman in the district. Up to that date there was no church nearer than St. Mary's, Plaistow, of which Mr. Marsh was vicar. But in that year some of the leading employers of labour in the neighbourhood, amongst whom may be mentioned Mr. William Cory and Lieutenant-Colonel Capper, manager of the Victoria Docks, subscribed sufficient money to build a small iron church on the North Woolwich Road, not far from the dock entrance. The

---

* This is the Rev. R. W. B. Marsh, whose name has already been mentioned in connection with Plaistow, and who is still living at Foulness Rectory, Southend.

clergyman's stipend was paid by the Plaistow and Victoria Dock Mission. The population of the district numbered at that time between four and five thousand souls. Mr. Douglas, after two years' hard work, was driven to despair by the poverty of his parishioners, and made an appeal to the *Times.*

His letter appeared on Christmas Eve, December 24, 1859, under the heading of "Londoners Over the Border," for which title he acknowledged his indebtedness to Charles Dickens' article in *Household Words.* It was a powerful appeal, the wretchedness of the locality being painted, if possible, in still more lurid colours than those the great novelist employed. The district was occupied, he wrote, chiefly by works for transforming the refuse of slaughter-houses into manure, and for the manufacture of vitriol and creosote.

The habitable area consisted of islands of liquid filth, surrounded by stagnant dikes, though with proper drainage it might be made as salubrious as Stepney or Pimlico.* Poverty alternated with fever. Every gust of prosperity brought an influx of strangers to the neighbourhood ; every succeeding stagnation overwhelmed the district with destitution. At the time of writing, the cry for food and fire was frightful. Amongst other distressing cases of illness, three whole families were down with fever, and in one day no less than seven accidents had occurred.

Mr. Douglas's letter was made the subject of the leading article on Christmas Day 1859. "Never in this world," the article began, "existed such prosperity, comfort, and happiness as are brought by this Christmas to hundreds of thousands of homes." Out of the three million inhabitants then resident in London, there must be many, the writer declared, who would willingly come forward to help their less fortunate fellow citizens in the East of the metropolis.

The letter and article met with a speedy response, and on January 9th, 1860, Mr. Douglas wrote to the *Times* acknowledging the receipt of various sums, which were more than sufficient for his present needs. As, however, his

* In those days Stepney and Pimlico were evidently regarded as pleasant country suburbs, to which jaded Londoners, worn out with work, withdrew to recuperate their strength.

temporary iron church lacked sufficient accommodation for the growing population, he had obtained leave from the Bishop of London to start a fund for a more permanent building. This second appeal was met in an equally generous manner, and on the following Christmas Eve, 1860, Mr. Douglas was able to announce that the subscriptions reached the handsome total of £14,000, including donations for a new church, new schools, and a parsonage.

The site chosen for the new church, instead of being in the populous district of Hallsville and Canning Town, was at the eastern end of the Victoria Docks, close to the isolated little settlement which had grown up round Silver's works. As the Dock Company presented the ground, no one else had a voice in the matter, and the directors could better afford to part with land at the deserted eastern end of their property than in the busy western quarter.

The spot selected certainly had its disadvantages. From Hallsville and Canning Town it could only be reached by crossing the swing bridge over the entrance to the Docks, and taking the North Woolwich Road by the side of the old railway on the south of the Docks. This was a private road built by the Land Company, and neither lighted nor kept in proper repair. The inhabitants of Custom House, in order to get to the church, would have to climb a number of fences and trespass on the North Woolwich Railway. When one of his parishioners remarked on the isolation of the site, Mr. Douglas replied, "Wait for a few years, and you will see that it is not so ill-chosen after all!" The clergyman's forecast has since been fully justified.

At the time, however, the selection of the site met with a good deal of hostile criticism. Even Messrs. Silvers had no reason to be grateful for its proximity, as they had already built a large schoolroom, in which service was held every Sunday. The scripture reader whom they engaged was Mr. E. H. Hopkins, now vicar of St. Luke's, Redcliffe Square. In the schoolroom during the week-days, not only the children of the workmen, but in the evening, many of the workmen themselves, whose education had been neglected, received instruction. Colonel Hugh Adams Silver, of Abbey Lodge, Chislehurst, to whom the writer is indebted for his information concerning the early days of the firm, remembers the difficulties of teaching these adults scholars to read and write. One father of a numerous family, when learning his lesson from the child's first book, would persist in saying that m, u, g spelt "pot," because the representation given of it resembled the familiar pewter of the public-house, rather than the china mug of the domestic table.

Many of the poor people, whom Mr. Douglas had relieved out of the money sent to him in response to his first appeal, turned against him when they found that the money from the second appeal was going towards the building of a church instead of affording them further assistance. Their case was taken up by a man named James Scully, residing in Canning Town, who, as the self-constituted champion of the parishioners, wrote a letter to the *Daily Telegraph* complaining, not, perhaps, inappositely, that they had asked for "bread," and Mr. Douglas was for giving them a "stone," in the form of his new church. Scully even accused the clergyman of misappropriating the funds intrusted to him. Mr. Douglas at once wrote to Lieut.-Colonel Capper, manager of the Docks, giving vouchers for the money he had spent. The colonel's reply, which, with Mr. Douglas's letter, was published in the *Times*, stated that the vouchers were quite satisfactory, and expressed a conviction that the clergyman was doing a great deal of good in the district.

This letter failed to silence Scully, and Mr. Douglas, for his own satisfaction, appealed to Dr. Tait, then Bishop of London, to appoint a commission of inquiry into the matter. Dr. Tait applied to two representative citizens of London, Mr. George Moore of Cheapside and Alderman Dakin, afterwards Lord Mayor, asking them to make the required investigation. They accepted the task, and on February 4, 1861, their report was published in the *Times*. They found that, out of the total sum of £14,200 14s. 4d., mentioned by Mr. Douglas as the amount of the fund, £11,070 had merely been promised and not paid. In the distribution of the relief fund they stated that there was an absence of systematic book-keeping. Mr. Douglas, however, possessed a private income of £1,000 in addition to his stipend of £100. He lived in a house in Custom House Terrace, the rent of which was only £25 per annum, and though his domestic expenditure did not exceed £600, his entire income had been disbursed. It was thus clear that, so far from having appropriated funds from other sources, he had actually been spending £400 per annum of his own money among his parishioners. The report concluded with a hope that Mr. Douglas might be spared "for many years to labour in the district."

This report might naturally have been expected to put an end to the calumnies of the reverend gentleman's traducers, but they were still continued. Unfortunately, his lack of proper book-keeping had, in reality, left some of the fund money unaccounted for, and he took the wiser course, resigning his appointment, and accepting the incumbency of Newborough, North Hants.

Mr. Douglas finally became rector of Edmondthorpe, Oakham, where he died as recently as 1897. Though belonging to a German Jewish family, which had assumed the name of Douglas, and himself associated in his early days with Dr. Cumming of Crown Court Chapel, the Presbyterian minister who foretold the end of the world, there was no reason to doubt the sincerity of his attachment to the English Church. His wife was the widow of Colonel Maclean and niece of the Earl of Cadogan. Miss Maclean, who lived with her mother and step-father at Custom House, and was noted for her beauty, subsequently married Canon Wilberforce.

Mrs. Talbot, of 281, Victoria Dock Road, a resident at Custom House of forty-five years' standing, has given the author some particulars of the early history of the neighbourhood. Mr. Talbot, manager of H. P. Burt and Co.'s Creosote Works in the Victoria Docks, was drowned during a fog in January, 1860. Mr. Douglas mentioned the fact in a letter which he wrote to the *Times*, dated Jan. 13th, 1860, when he appealed for funds in aid of his widow and children. On her husband's death, Mrs. Talbot was given charge of a needlewomen's institute, formed by Mr. Douglas to assist the poor women of the neighbourhood. They used to make shirts for the Army and Navy, obtaining, now and again, orders for as many as 4,000 at a time. Glove-making and wood-chopping were also undertaken, to give employment to women who had no other means of earning money for their families. Custom House Terrace, now taken by the

Ashburnham Mission, was built in 1855. Mr. Douglas
lived in the corner house at the western end, and one of
the row was occupied by Mr. Collins, a chemist, who,
having failed in business, became station-master at Custom
House Station. With him lodged at one time Mr. Bidder
the "calculating boy."

During the disputes about the building of St. Mark's
Church, Silvertown, in 1861, Mr. Morrison, chairman of
the Victoria Dock Company, erected the small Church of
St. Matthew's, close to Custom House Station. A year
later, on August 17, 1862, St. Mark's Church was con-
secrated by the Bishop of London. The Rev. Henry Boyd,
now Dr. Boyd, and Principal of Hertford College, Oxford,
was the first incumbent. Mr. Boyd lived in Custom House
Terrace till St. Mark's Parsonage was ready for occupation
in February, 1865. The new clergyman was an indefatigable
worker in the parish, receiving great help from his sister,
Miss Louisa Boyd.

In those days, when the neighbourhood was full of
disorderly characters, the policeman conspicuously absent,
and the houses few and far between, it required some
courage, even in a man, to walk about the ill-lighted roads
after dark. Miss Boyd never allowed such fears to deter
her from the execution of her parish work, though during
the garotting scare she confesses to having purchased a
revolver and taken a little quiet practice on the marshes as
a mere precautionary measure. A difficulty arose when the
fences on the way to the church had to be surmounted with
a fully-loaded revolver. On such occasions Miss Talbot,
who often accompanied Miss Boyd, would be entrusted
with the dangerous weapon till the fence had been successfully scaled.

Miss Boyd was a member of the West Ham School
Board from its inception till the last election, when she took
upon herself a similar office for Wanstead. She had been
the only lady on the West Ham Board, and as one of the
electors remarked, owing to her thorough practical know-
ledge of the work, was worth more than all the men put
together. Miss Boyd, who now lives at Wanstead, still
continues to visit her old district one day in every week.

St. Mark's Church, in the short period of fifteen years,

Photo by]

Landing Shore End at Bacton, Norfolk.

[C. R. Wylie, Esq.

[To face

belonged in succession to no less than three episcopal dioceses. At its consecration in 1862, being in the parish of St. Mary's, Plaistow, it came within the jurisdiction of the Bishop of London. In what year the Bishop of London took Plaistow into his fold does not appear. According to "White's Gazetteer" published 1848, Plaistow, together with all the parishes in the half hundred of Becontree, belonged to the diocese of Rochester. Perhaps someone discovered that a mistake had been made, for in 1872 St. Mark's was handed over to the bishopric of Rochester. The change was a loss to Silvertown, for the incumbent ceased to have any claim on the rich Bishop of London's Fund. The transfer was effected when Dr. Tait became Archbishop of Canterbury.

For five years the parish remained in the diocese of Rochester, Mr. Boyd becoming a canon of that bishopric; then, in 1879, the new diocese of St. Albans was created, and to it were transferred all the parishes in Essex, Hertford and Kent, north of the river, which had belonged to Rochester. Dr. Claughton, then Bishop of Rochester was given his choice of remaining at Rochester or taking St. Albans. So far from claiming both, like the celebrated bishop of Bath and Wells, Dr. Claughton was content to accept the new and presumably minor bishopric of St. Albans.

During his incumbency at Silvertown, Dr. Boyd was instrumental in building no less than two other churches, with church schools attached. In September, 1872, St. John's, North Woolwich, was completed, and two years later St. Luke's, Victoria Docks, was built. The first vicar of St. Luke's was the Rev. Thomas Stevens, previously curate of St. Marks, and now Archdeacon Stevens, vicar of St. John the Evangelist, Stratford. Mr. J. A. Phillips, from whom the writer received a good deal of information concerning the district, was made head-master of St. Luke's National School, a post which he holds to the present day.

With regard to St. John's Church, North Woolwich, Mr. Curwen states, in his "Old Plaistow," that having been built on marshland, which shrank and contracted when the marshes were drained, the piles which had been driven into the ground for its support, thrust their heads through the floor, and had to be sawn off. A publichouse in the Victoria Dock Road for the same reason was said to have sunk three feet.

Dr. Boyd, to the general regret of the district, left St. Mark's, Victoria Docks, in January, 1875, having been appointed Dean of Hertford College, Oxford. He became Principal in May, 1877.

CHAPTER IX.

Growth of Messrs. Silver & Co.'s Works—Submarine Cables—Mr. W. T. Henley's Telegraph Works—Northern Outfall Sewer—Beckton Gas Works—Bermuda Floating Dock—The Great Eastern—Royal Albert Dock.

MESSRS. SILVER'S works had by this time increased to such an extent, and had gathered round them so many residents, as to justify the name of Silvertown being given to the district of which they formed the centre. Beginning with waterproof clothing and belting for machinery, the manufacture of other kinds of rubber goods, including ebonite, was soon undertaken. Ebonite is hardened rubber, made by prolonging or intensifying the curing or vulcanising process. "The method of its manufacture was discovered," Colonel Silver says, "in a curious manner. Hollow india-rubber balls are made out of sheet rubber, cut in two sections and inflated by oxalic acid in a bath of melted sulphur. During the process one of the balls fell unnoticed to the bottom of the bath. When found at the end of the week it had hardened into ebonite."

Ebonite is an invaluable substance. Its qualities are hardness, elasticity and non-porosity. It has replaced wood in numberless articles, because it does not warp with moisture. Before its discovery vinegar manufacturers had constant trouble from the corrosion of their metal pumps and pipes. Now all their utensils are made of ebonite, on which vinegar has no effect. On account of its resistance to chemical action, it is indispensable in the laboratory, and its electrical non-conductivity makes it invaluable as the basis of all electrical instruments.

The growth of Messrs. Silver's works was so satisfactory that in 1864 a prospectus was issued for converting the business into a company, under the title of "Silver's India-rubber Works and Telegraph Cable Company, Limited."

On the Provisional Committee, amongst other well-known names, were those of Sam Mendel of Manchester, and William Fenton of the Great Western Railway. Colonel H. A. Silver* and J. W. Willans were the first managing directors, but they retired a year after the formation of the company, and Mr. Mathew Gray became sole managing director. The india-rubber and gutta-percha departments had been under separate management from the time that Mr. Hancock, gutta-percha manufacturer at Smithfield, amalgamated with Messrs. Silvers, and brought his own engineers and workmen with him. The two departments were now put under the sole direction of Mr. Mathew Gray, and it is to his untiring energy and excellent capacity for business that the firm owes its present prosperous position.

Mr. Gray soon turned his attention to the manufacture of submarine cables, and in 1867, only a year after the laying of the first successful Atlantic cable, he obtained an order from the Western Union Telegraph Company of America for a cable to connect Key West, the southernmost point of the United States, with Havana. Sir Charles Bright, who laid the first though unsuccessful Atlantic cable in 1858, was the engineer selected by the company to carry out their contract.

The cable between Havana and Key West, which was the first to be made and laid by the company, is still working, in spite of having been immersed thirty-one years in the water. It was repaired as recently as 1899 by S.S. *Dacia*. The *Dacia*, built in the early sixties for the Mediterranean

---

* Colonel H. A. Silver raised the Silvertown Rifle Corp in 1859, retiring in 1889, after thirty years' work, with a long-service medal. From this corps has sprung the present 4th Volunteer Battalion of the Essex Regiment, which has its head-quarters at Silvertown, and sent over 50 men to South Africa against the Boers. East and West Ham have always been loyal to the Crown, and Mr. S. B. Boulton possesses a medal struck by Sir John Henniker, Bart., in connection with "The Loyal West and East Ham Volunteers, associated May 18th, 1798." Sir John, who lived at Stratford House, Maryland Point, chose for the motto "*Deus major columna*," "The Lord is mightier than a host," and added the Greek words, τοῦ ἀριστεύειν ἕνεκὰ, signifying that it was given as a proof of excellence. The choice of the Greek preposition ἕνεκὰ (pronounced henneker) looks as if Sir John cast about for a play of words on his own name. On the medal also appears the following : "For the maintenance of internal peace for King and constitution."

fruit trade, was acquired in 1869 by Sir Charles Bright. In order to increase her carrying capacity he lengthened her by 40 feet cutting her in two and inserting that amount of hull at her waist. She was purchased by the Silvertown Company in 1870. The *Dacia* is the *doyen* of cable ships, and her cable machinery, though designed and made so many years ago, is still as good as that of any cable ship afloat.

In 1870-71 followed the West India and Panama cables, which, owing to the rocky character of the sea bottom, gave a great deal of trouble in the laying. Yellow fever also attacked the ship, every fifth man on board succumbing to it. A more pleasant task was the laying of the Algiers-Marseilles cable for the French Government in 1871, and the Lizard-Bilbao cable in 1872.

About this time the company acquired S.S. *International*, and fitted her with cable tanks and the requisite machinery. The first cable she laid was in 1870, between the Channel Islands and the English coast. In 1899, having retired from active service for several years, the *International* was sold to a Frenchman, who tried to tow her to Boulogne. But a fresh breeze sprang up, the hawser parted, and the old ship went ashore at Beachy Head, at the very spot from which she had laid one of her first cables. Her bare ribs now gaze regretfully upon the scene of her early labours.

In 1875-6 the West Coast of America cables, a total of some 1,700 knots, were laid. On the way out the *Dacia* met, anchored in Smyth's Channel, the *Sunbeam*, then on the voyage with which Lady Brassey has familiarised the world. The encounter is described in the pages of her book. Smaller cables in such different quarters of the globe as the Caspian Sea, the Gulf of Florida, and the Canadian coast followed, and then the company received an order for over 3,000 knots of cable to be laid on the West Coast of Central and South America.

To execute this order the telegraph steamship *Hooper* was acquired from Messrs. Hooper, telegraph engineers, and re-christened the *Silvertown*. She was the first ship to be designed expressly as a cable ship. The story is that the cable engineer responsible for her drew three circles representing the diameter and depth of the cable tanks he wanted, and the naval architect was instructed to build

a ship around them. When launched she was, with the
exception of the *Great Eastern*, the largest cargo ship afloat,
and her cable tanks were actually one third larger than
those of the leviathan. In the intervals between cable-
laying the *Silvertown* has carried general cargo, and on one
occasion brought from New Orleans the largest load of
grain that has ever crossed the Atlantic. It was at the end
of this voyage that a paltry 300 tons of sugar could not be
found, till a supercargo stumbled accidentally upon them
in one of her capacious pockets. During the Chilian Civil
War in 1891, she was present at the bombardment of
Iquique, and gave a temporary home to a number of English women and children who were driven from the town.

A fourth cable-ship, the *Buccaneer*, was acquired by the
company in 1885. Though only a small vessel, she has
done a good deal of useful work in water too shallow for
larger ships, and also in repairs.

In much the same way as Silvertown owes its existence
to Mr. Silver's works, the growth of North Woolwich is
identified with Mr. Henley's works. Mr. W. T. Henley
was born at Midhurst in 1814, and began life as a leather
dresser. In 1830 he came to London and took the situation
of a light porter at a silk mercer's in Cheapside. He then
worked for five years in the Docks, during which he taught
himself the use of tools and made electrical instruments.
This brought him at the age of 24 to the notice of Wheat-
stone, who engaged his services. Whilst working with him,
Mr. Henley invented a magnetic telegraph, subsequently
promoting a company, which purchased the patent for
£68,000 in cash and shares. This company laid underground lines from London to Carlisle, and from Dublin to
Belfast, in opposition to the old Electric Company.

In 1853, one year after Mr. Silver had bought his land at
Silvertown, Mr. Henley acquired twelve acres at North
Woolwich, on which he built works for the manufacture of
submarine cables and electrical apparatus generally. Four
years later he obtained the contract for a cable between
India and Ceylon, and in 1865 laid the shore end of the
successful Atlantic cable at Valencia, handing over the sea-
ward end to be spliced on board the *Great Eastern*. The
works were very successful till Mr. Henley attempted to

[Photo by]

[C. R. Wylie, Esq.

Horses hauling Cable ashore at Bacton, Norfolk.

[To face p.

draw his own sheathing wire, an undertaking in which he could not compete with northern firms on account of the cost of coal. The business failed and a company was formed, Mr. Henley becoming manager of the submarine department. He died in 1882. In 1874 North Woolwich suffered severely in the wreck of Henley's telegraph steamer *La Plata*, only 17 lives being saved out of a total of 75 on board.

A great engineering work in the neighbourhood of Silvertown and North Woolwich, namely, the construction of the Northern Outfall Sewer, was successfully completed in 1863. Its object was to carry the sewage of north London into the Thames at a suitable distance below the metropolis. The embankment begins at Victoria Park, crosses the River Lea at Old Ford, runs under the Great Eastern main line between Stratford and Coburn Road, is carried over the Channelsea at Abbey Mills, and, after traversing Plaistow and East Ham levels, reaches the river on the western bank of Barking Creek.

Three channels, 9 feet in diameter, are contained in the embankment. Till 1889 the sewage used to pass unchanged into the Thames when the tide was on the ebb, but as a result of a Royal Commission in 1882 clarifying works were instituted. They cover an area of 83 acres, and treat the whole of North London sewage, which flows by gravity from the Abbey Pumping Station at Stratford. The clarification is effected by a chemical process, which is calculated to cost $4\frac{1}{2}d.$ per ton of sludge precipitated. The sludge is carried out to sea by six steamers of 1,000 tons each, which also serve the Southern Outfall Works at Crossness. Works are in progress at West Ham for pumping the sewage of the district into the Northern Outfall Sewer.

In 1868 the Gas Light and Coke Company bought 500 acres of land between the Northern Outfall Sewer, Manor Way and the River Thames. The Gas Light and Coke Company is the oldest gas company in existence, being formed as early as 1809, and obtaining a charter the following year to supply with gas "the cities of London and Westminster." The first street lighted by them was Pall Mall, in 1809. The new illuminant met with vigorous opposition at the first, scientists making fun of it, and the great Sir

Humphrey Davy himself humorously proposing that the dome of St. Paul's should be used as a gasometer. The more nervous prophesied a series of terrible explosions, though, as a matter of fact, no gasometer was destroyed in this way till the explosion at Nine Elms in 1869.

The works at Beckton—so called after Mr. S. A. Beck, governor of the company when the land was purchased—are the largest in the world. They can supply more than half of the maximum daily output of the nine stations belonging to the company, and this output is equal to one-fifth of the gas supply of the United Kingdom. The primary object of their erection was to provide gas for the West End, and two mains, 4 feet in diameter, run from Beckton through London to Kensal Green. The cost of laying these huge mains for such a distance has been amply repaid by the cheapness of the land and facilities for obtaining seaborne coal which the locality afforded.

Beckton Gasworks possess two piers with berths for six steam colliers of 2,000 tons, and thirty locomotives of standard gauge to take the coal to the retorts. A private line to Custom House and a private road to Canning Town also belong to the company. The works include a village of 130 cottages, besides larger houses, a church, chapel, institute, canteen and recreation ground. They contribute one-half of the total rateable value of Barking, in which district the major portion of them lies.

In spite of C. J. Mare's failure, and the ill-success of the company which first succeeded him, Messrs. Campbell, Johnstone and Co. were venturesome enough in the early sixties to set up a shipbuilding yard on the eastern side of Messrs. Silver's works. Here H.M.S. *Resistance*, the fourth ironclad ordered by the navy, was built, but the work by which the yard will be chiefly remembered was the Bermuda Floating Dock. The porous nature of the rock of which Bermuda is composed rendered a land dock impossible, and a floating dock was therefore ordered. Mr. James Campbell, senior partner in the firm, who had been engaged in the erection of the Menai Tubular Bridge, prepared and patented the plans, which were adapted by Colonel Clarke, R.E., for the special requirements of Bermuda Harbour.

The Bermuda Dock, besides being far larger than any

other floating dock of the time, was the only one put together in England, those at Sargon, Carthagena, Cadiz, and Callao having been sent out in sections. With a length of 381 feet and an inside width of 84 feet, she was designed to take ironclads of 10,000 tons displacement. She is now only the seventh largest floating dock in the world, one at Hamburg being no less than 560 feet long and 88 feet wide.

A great deal of interest was taken in the building of the Bermuda Dock, which commenced in August, 1866, and both the Prince of Wales and the Duke of Cambridge came down to inspect her. The launch was announced for September 2, 1868, and a distinguished company were invited to witness it. Unfortunately the dock, which had a dead weight of some 10,000 tons, refused to move, and after many vain efforts to set her going, the attempt was abandoned for the day. There was no reason, however, why the lunch which had been prepared in honour of the occasion should not be eaten, and this function, at any rate, passed off successfully, those who had come with ready-made speeches skilfully adapting them to the altered circumstances.

The Bermuda Dock was finally launched without much trouble, in which respect she was more lucky than H.M.S. *Northumberland*, which, together with the *Warrior*, towed her to Madeira. The *Northumberland*, built by Mr. Mare's Millwall Company, required four weeks' continuous work, day and night, to launch her, and cost £12,000 in the process. Still more unfortunate was the *Great Eastern*, the launch of which was attempted on November 3, 1857, and not accomplished till January 31, 1858

In the case of the *Great Eastern*, the failure was attributed by Mr. Scott Russell, the builder, to the fact that Brunel, the designer, who was a strong believer in iron, insisted on laying down iron ways instead of wooden ways, on which to launch her. The ship slid a few feet till the lubricating grease was expended, and then iron bit iron, like the wheels of a locomotive on the rails. Though the incline was 1 in 12, it took nearly three months, with some thousands of tons pressure from hydraulic rams, to force her down to the water. The reason for launching her broadside, was that if she had been built end on, her great

G

length would have carried the fore part of her keel some thirty feet above the ground level, and a good distance inland beyond the limits of the builders' premises.

In 1864, the *Great Eastern* was bought by Glass, Elliot & Co., and two years later laid the first successful Atlantic cable. The French Atlantic cable followed in 1869, and the fourth and fifth cables in 1873 and 1874 respectively. In 1885 she was sold for £26,200, and kept on show in the Mersey till October 12, 1886. Finally, this magnificent ship, which cost £732,000 to build, was knocked down to Henry Bath & Sons, metal brokers, for £16,500—less than a fortieth of her original value—and broken up by them.

In pleasing contrast to these unsuccessful launches, for the account of which the writer is indebted to Mr. Mackrow's reminiscences, may be mentioned the case of H.M.S. *Thunder*, built in Mare's yard in 1856. This vessel launched herself while the men were having breakfast on the very day appointed for the ceremony, and, what is still more strange, did not do the slightest damage to herself or anyone else.

The success of the Victoria Docks led to the formation of the Royal Albert Docks. As early as 1864 land had been bought for the purpose, but the original intention had been merely to make an easterly entrance to the Victoria Docks by a canal which would cut off Woolwich Reach. This idea was subsequently abandoned in favour of a basin, 500 feet wide and over a mile in length, which would also serve the purposes of a dock.

The bankruptcy of the contractor, Sir Morton Peto, threw back the work for a considerable time, and it was not till 1880 that the Albert Docks were finally opened. The first outlet was built on a sandbank, and gave a great deal of trouble, eventually necessitating the formation of another entrance to the eastward at a cost of £200,000. The Victoria and Albert Docks together are 2¾ miles in length. The channel connecting the two cut the North Woolwich Railway at a point about half-way between Custom House and Silvertown. To avoid this channel a tunnel beneath the eastern end of the Victoria Docks was built.

Until the opening of the Albert Docks the only road

from Silvertown to London was the North Woolwich Road, to the south of the Victoria Docks. This road, as already stated, belonged to the Land Company, who placed a toll-gate on it. The extension of the Victoria Dock Road from Custom House *viâ* Connaught Road Station to Silvertown gave an alternative route to town. This induced the Land Company to remove their tollgate to a spot near the present post-office, so as to command both routes. Their action was opposed by Mr. Wilton, manager of the Silvertown branch of the Gas Light and Coke Company, who forcibly removed it, and eventually compelled the Land Company to abandon the idea.

CHAPTER X.

Tate's Sugar Refinery—Abram Lyle & Sons—Keiller's Marmalade—
William Cory & Son, Ltd.—The India-rubber, Gutta-percha, and
Telegraph Works Co., Ltd.

SINCE the opening of the Albert Docks, Silvertown has grown apace. There are now, at least, twenty large firms—not to mention smaller ones—on its river frontage, which extends from West Ham Pumping Station to the entrance to the Victoria Docks. Chemical, creosoting, and manure works alternate with jam, soap, and sugar manufactories. Tate's and Lyle's are the principal representatives of the sugar industry at Silvertown. The firm of Henry Tate & Co. was originally located in Liverpool, having taken over the business of John Wright & Co., sugar refiners, in 1862. In order to develop the cube-sugar trade, the patent for which they possessed, they came to London in 1877, and bought the land once occupied by Campbell, Johnstone & Co.'s shipbuilding yard, adjoining the premises of the Telegraph Works Company.

Although everybody is familiar with the name of Tate's cube sugar, few understand the reason why it has won its present leading position in the sugar trade. Previous to the cube patent, which was taken out in 1876, sugar used to be manufactured in large cones or loaves, called, for some unknown reason, "titlers." These titlers were bought by grocers and cut up by hand with a long knife hinged at one end, and familiarly known as the "guillotine." The process was laborious and wasteful, and the cube patent did away with it by manufacturing sugar in small ready-made blocks or cubes. The new article encountered considerable opposition at first amongst grocers, who regarded the cutting up of sugar as a useful occupation for their assistants when they had nothing else to do. But it was soon found out that the extra 2s. a cwt. which cube sugar cost,

Photo by]

Testing-room on board s.s. "Buccaneer."

[E. Raymond-Barker, Esq.

[To face p. 84.

was more than covered by the saving of time and labour effected by it.

A patent is said to be of little use till it has been upheld in the Law Courts, and Henry Tate & Co. obtained the confirmation of their patent for cube sugar in 1882, when they won their case against the French firm of Say & Co., of Paris. Their position thus secured, an enormous business was developed. The output at Silvertown has risen from 600 tons per week in 1878 to 2,000 tons per week at the present time, and the firm employs some five or six hundred men. Sir Henry Tate died in the latter part of 1899 leaving £1,263,365, of which a sum of £50,000 was devoted to charity. In his lifetime the Tate Institute for working men had been erected at Silvertown, and the Tate Picture Gallery made over to the nation.

Abram Lyle & Sons came from Greenock, where they were originally timber merchants, making, amongst other articles, boxes and casks for sugar refiners. In 1862, the same year in which the Tates took over John Wright's business, the Lyles bought up a bankrupt customer, and embarked in the sugar trade. At one time they also owned a line of sailing ships, called the Cape Line. In 1881 the business was removed to Silvertown. Lyle & Sons turn out some 1,800 tons of sugar a week, but they are best known in connection with Lyle's golden syrup, which, though never advertised, has won great popularity, owing to its superior refinement and the portability of the tins in which it is sold.

Whilst on the subject of sugar, mention must be made of James Keiller & Son, of Dundee marmalade fame. They have a factory adjacent to the Telegraph Works, where, in addition to marmalade, cocoa and various kinds of jam are made. The late head of the firm died in 1899, leaving a very considerable fortune.

Next to Silver's, Odams' Chemical Manure Works are the oldest on the river front, Mr. Odams having acquired as early as 1852 the ground on which they stand, to the east of the entrance to the Victoria Docks. The land was bought from Mr. Hudson, a wealthy Bond Street butcher, who owned Cumberland House, Plaistow, and a good deal of the surrounding marshland on which he fed his cattle.

Mr. Hudson used to supply Prince George of Wales, afterwards George IV., with meat, and found great difficulty in
getting his money, the account sometimes running up to a
thousand pounds. The successful butcher retired to
Cumberland House in his old age, and died there.

In 1866, when the rinderpest was introduced into England,
by imported cattle, Mr. Odams bought fifteen additional
acres of ground on the river front, and made a wharf and
landing stage, lairs for resting the cattle, a place for
marketing, and slaughter-houses. He then tendered them
to the Privy Council, with the result that an order was
issued compelling all foreign cattle to be landed, marketed,
and slaughtered at this spot. The business was converted
into a company in 1856, and now turns out some 35,000
tons per annum of nitrates, phosphates, and super-phos-
phates for land manures.

Messrs. Burt, Boulton & Haywood, Ltd.—formerly H. P.
Burt & Co.—manufacturers of coal-tar products and railway
timber, took their present premises in the Victoria Docks
as soon as the docks were opened in 1855. In 1870 they
acquired Prince Regent's Wharf on the river front. The
company now have works at Ealing, Newport, Cardiff, West
Hartlepool, Selzatte in Belgium, Bilbao in Spain, and
Bordeaux in the south of France. Their next-door neigh-
bours, Messrs. Spencer, Chapman & Messel, Ltd., are the
largest acid manufacturers on the Thames. They were
the first firm in the world to produce on a manufacturing
scale sulphuric anhydride, by a catalytic process invented
by Dr. Messel and Mr. Squire, and by subsequent improvements to extend this manufacture to the production of
ordinary or commercial sulphuric acid.

Messrs. John Knight & Sons are the owners of the
Silvertown Soap Works. Soap, although the chief, is by no
means the only product of this manufactory. After being
boiled, the oil of the best beef fat is separated from the
stearine or solid matter by hydraulic pressure. The stearine
is made into candles. The oil, such as is not retained for
the manufacture of the best kind of soap, is sent abroad to
be made into oleomargarine. The glycerine developed in
the saponification process, which formerly was allowed to
run to waste, is now recovered and used in the production

of nitro-glycerine and dynamite. Resin being one of the constituents of soap, thousands of barrels are imported yearly from North Carolina. For the production of soft soap the firm make their own cotton-seed oil, importing the best Egyptian cotton seed for the purpose. The solid residue of the seed is made up into oil-cakes for animals; the oil itself is used for frying fish, and for the manufacture of butterine in France and Holland. The firm employ some 500 hands and have 80 to 90 horses in their stables.

William Griffiths, paviors and contractors, acquired their wharf and adjoining land at North Woolwich in 1889. Their other depôts are at Devonshire Street, Tufnell Park, Kingsland, and Palace Gates. Guernsey, Norway, Sweden, and Scotland supply them with granite for road-making, and the material for wood pavements comes from West Australia. A mill in their yard is capable of turning out 60,000 blocks of wood a day. The paving of Regent Street with wood was one of their contracts, and they built nearly the whole of the North Metropolitan Tramway system. Their yearly output of coal and timber from North Woolwich is 150,000 tons.

Mention has already been made of the firm of William Cory & Son, and Mr. S. Mepham, their late manager, has kindly given the author some particulars of their more recent growth. By 1896 their business was of such dimensions that they decided to effect an amalgamation with other large merchants of seaborne coal, and a company was formed under the title of William Cory & Son, Ltd. In the association were included C. J. Cockerell, Green Holland & Sons, and J. & C. Harrison. In 1898 a third derrick was built, 500 feet in length, at which two steamers of 3,000 tons can be discharged in from fifteen to twenty hours. Nine travelling cranes weigh the coal at the same time as they transfer it into barges on the other side of the derrick. This derrick took the berth of the first derrick, which is now stationed at Erith. When a collier passes Tilbury the discharging station is informed by telegram, so that the men can be called out, ready to begin work, as soon as the vessel comes alongside.

William Cory & Sons, Ltd., possess a fleet of 45 colliers, of 2,000 to 3,000 tons, some 1,400 barges, and 25 tugs.

At Charlton they have a station for coaling tugs and river steamers, as well as the largest barge building yard in the United Kingdom. Their output is 5,000,000 tons a year. The firm has no connection with that of Cory Brothers, who are coal exporters. The present chairman is Mr. F. C Cory-Wright, who is closely identified with the success of the firm.

A brief survey of the position of the India-rubber, Gutta-percha and Telegraph Works Co., Ltd., who now employ between 2,700 and 3,000 men, must conclude this account of the various firms at Silvertown. The work of the Submarine Cable Department since 1883 includes the connecting of the Canary Islands with each other and with Cadiz. In 1885-89 the Cape Verde Islands and all the important towns on the West Coast of Africa as far as Mossamedes were put into communication with Europe, the connecting link from Mossamedes to Cape Town providing a much-needed alternative route to the Cape. The cable system on both the East and West Coasts of America was extended in 1890-91, and in 1892 an Atlantic cable was laid from St. Louis, Senegal, *viâ* the island of Fernando Noronha, to Pernambuco in Brazil. In 1897-98 the company laid the new French Atlantic cable from Brest to Cape Cod, the longest cable in the world, being 2,800 nautical miles in length. The total amount of cable made at Silvertown is approximately forty thousand miles.

The laying of a cable entails a good deal more work than the mere steaming from one to the other of the two stations which are to be connected by it. During each step in the manufacture—the covering with gutta-percha of the copper wire or conductor, through which the electric current passes, and the sheathing with steel wires of the core thus made—constant tests are taken. Before laying, the intended route is carefully sounded, to discover any irregularities in the sea bottom which would be injurious to the cable. The sounder is lowered at the end of a long coil of fine pianoforte wire, wound on a drum, the heavy shot used for sinking it being automatically released on reaching the bottom so as to facilitate the recovery of the sounder. The number of revolutions of the drum, recorded by an index attached to it, gives the depth to which the sounder has sunk.

On reaching the spot where the cable is to be landed, sheaved wheels are fixed on the beach, and a line passing round them and back to the ship hauls the end of the cable, floated by large india-rubber balloons, to the shore. The end is taken into a cable hut furnished with electrical instruments, and during‐the laying electricians remain in the hut to keep up communication day and night with the ship. In a depth of 2,000 fathoms, the cable takes about 3 hours to sink, so that if a ship is paying out at the rate of 9 knots an hour, the distance from the vessel to the spot where the cable reaches the bottom, is no less than 27 nautical miles.

Considerable skill is required for cable repairing, The fault is first localised by an electrician in a cable hut at one of the ends. The calculated distance to the fault— which is less than the length of cable to the fault, for the cable has a certain percentage of slack—is given to the captain, who must be an experienced navigator to bring his ship in mid-ocean to the required spot. A mark buoy is then lowered, and the work of grappling commences. If the depth is great, a cutting grapnel is often used, so that the cable may be recovered in two separate loose ends, instead of incurring the strain of bringing a bight of it up to the surface. The end of the sound piece of cable is buoyed, the fault is cut out of the other, and a new piece spliced in between the two points.

The other departments of the Silvertown Telegraph Works have enjoyed a steady flow of work. Amongst the countless purposes to which india-rubber is now applied, the earliest one on record still figures prominently. India-rubber balls are as much in demand amongst English boys as they were amongst the natives of Hayti when Columbus interrupted their sport by landing on their shores four centuries ago. In England, however, the first use to which the new material was put when introduced in 1772, was the rubbing out of pencil marks. In fact, india-rubber owes its name to what is now one of its smallest and least important functions.

Every kind of rubber ball is made at Silvertown. In point of numbers tennis balls head the list, though footballs show the respectable total of 600,000 in a season. The

well-known Silvertown golf-ball, of course, outnumbers both
together, but then it is made of gutta-percha, and not india-
rubber.

India-rubber was first used to make clothing waterproof
in 1820 by Mr. Macintosh, a Scotchman, whose name a
grateful, but misinformed, southern public perpetuate in
Mackintosh. Rubber, in the form of elastic, enters into
various articles of attire. It is the best material for tobacco
pouches, and in the house it is to be found in rubber
draught tubing for doors and windows, rubber sprays for
scent bottles, rubber bands for papers, and rubber rings for
aërated water bottles. In the form of ebonite it supplies
buttons, combs, paper-knives, pens, thimbles, and scores of
fancy articles, while ebonite screw stoppers for beer and
lemonade bottles are stamped out by the hundred gross at
Silvertown.

There is hardly a sport in which rubber or gutta-percha is
not represented. Cycling would be a poor recreation
without pneumatic tyres, and Silvertown manufactures the
well-known Palmer pattern. The works provide the angler
with his waterproof leggings, the yachtsman with his
rubber sea boots, and the sportsman with an ebonite heel-
plate for his gun. The tennis player is only half equipped
with tennis balls, for rubber-soled shoes are quite as
indispensable. The hunting-man wears a waterproof cover
coat, and the cricketer has rubber guards on the back of
his batting gloves. Billiards would be impossible without
rubber cushions, the cues are supported on ebonite rests, and
even the driver of a coach and four carries a whip with a
gutta-percha lash.

It is difficult to conceive how business could be carried
on without india-rubber and gutta-percha goods. Engines,
in addition to rubber valves and washers, require rubber
belting to transmit their energy. Railway carriages are
fitted with rubber buffers, and vacuum brakes are worked
with flexible rubber tubes. The Silvertown works provide
everything to do with electricity ; batteries, instruments,
and leads for telegraphic communication, and dynamos for
electric light. A modern steamer is full of its goods.
Rubber hoses pour water on its decks, and rubber
squeegees drive it off again. Rubber mats stand at the

Relaxation on the Cable Steamship "Silvertown." (Deck Quoits).

[*To face p. 90.*

top of the companion ways, and rubber tesselated pavement adorns the bathrooms. Electric bell-pushes are to be found in the cabins, electric bells in the stewards' quarters, and electric dynamos provide the electric lamps with light. Nervous passengers would do well to take the rubber pocket swimming collar, which can be dropped over the head and inflated in half-a-minute, and which when not in use occupies but a small space in the pocket.

In war time torpedoes manufactured by the company protect our harbours, and their cables give intimation of the movements of the enemy. Correspondents find the usefulness of waterproof knapsacks and hold-alls, nor do they despise the folding rubber bath. Photographers require ebonite trays, dippers, funnels and cups to develop and print their pictures. Telephones and electric bells are invaluable to connect the trenches round a beleaguered town.

The medical corps is supplied with bandages, hospital sheeting, rubber water bottles, cushions, pillows and beds. Ebonite forms the base of numberless medical instruments. But the brighter side of war is not neglected, and in the regimental bands ebonite bassoons, clarionets, oboes and piccolos help to cheer the soldier on his march, and after victory to make his pulse beat more quickly to the familiar, but well-loved, air, "God Save the Queen."

But little more need be said about the modern borough of West Ham, of which Silvertown is only one amongst thirteen polling districts. The river front of the wide expanse of marshland between Bow Creek and Barking Creek, on which in 1850 only two houses stood, is now lined with thriving manufactories. Behind them lie the Albert and Victoria Docks, affording berths for ships from every quarter of the globe. In addition to the works which have been mentioned West Ham contains two large engineering industries, the Great Eastern Railway Works at Stratford and the London Tilbury and Southend Railway Works at Plaistow. Till 1850, three churches sufficed for the needs of the population; the old parish church of All Saints, West Ham, St. John's, Stratford, and St. Mary's, Plaistow. Now there are twenty-six edifices belonging to the Church of England, exclusive of mission churches and places of worship devoted to other denominations. The small town of 18,000 inhabitants in 1850 has become a prosperous borough of 300,000 inhabitants in 1900. We are accustomed to hear of the rapid growth of cities in America and the Colonies, yet few can equal this marvellous development which has been going on at home, beneath, as it were, our very eyes.

INDEX.